More Praise for *Disagreements, Disputes, and All-Out War*

"Scott lays out a simple—but not simplistic—approach to conflict resolution. She provides lots of examples, assessments, and ideas that should help anyone who even takes a little time to read and apply her method."

—Rick Maurer, author of *Why Don't You Want What I Want?*

"The book provides us with clear directions on how to resolve all kinds of personal and business conflicts, drawing upon a comprehensive array of practical, academic, and intuitive resources."

—Shari Dunn, Managing Principal, CompAnalysis

"Gini's ERI Method is a gift to anyone searching for an explicit, step-by-step approach to minimizing conflict in their life—by adjusting the one thing we can all control—our own perspective."

—Andrea M. Eichorn, JD, Mediator and Collaborative Attorney

Disagreements, Disputes, and
All-Out War

3 Simple Steps for
Dealing with Any Kind of Conflict

Gini Graham Scott, Ph.D.

AMACOM
American Management Association
New York • Atlanta • Brussels • Chicago • Mexico City • San Francisco
Shanghai • Tokyo • Toronto • Washington, D.C.

Special discounts on bulk quantities of AMACOM books are
available to corporations, professional associations, and other
organizations. For details, contact Special Sales Department,
AMACOM, a division of American Management Association,
1601 Broadway, New York, NY 10019.
Tel: 212–903–8316. Fax: 212–903–8083.
E-mail: specialsls@amanet.org
Website: www. amacombooks.org/go/specialsales
To view all AMACOM titles go to: www.amacombooks.org

*This publication is designed to provide accurate and authoritative
information in regard to the subject matter covered. It is sold with the
understanding that the publisher is not engaged in rendering legal,
accounting, or other professional service. If legal advice or other expert
assistance is required, the services of a competent professional person
should be sought.*

Library of Congress Cataloging-in-Publication Data

Scott, Gini Graham.
    Disagreements, disputes, and all-out war : 3 simple steps for dealing with any kind of
conflict / Gini Graham Scott.
        p.   cm.
    Includes bibliographical references and index.
    ISBN-13: 978–0-8144–8063–2
    ISBN-10: 0–8144–8063–2
    1. Conflict management. 2. Interpersonal conflict. 3. Conflict (Psychology). I. Title.

HD42.S356   2008
303.6'9—dc22   2007017660

Printing number

10   9   8   7   6   5   4   3   2   1

To everyone who has shared their conflicts
with me in seeking assistance.

Helping them resolve their conflicts helped me to develop
the conflict resolution model described in this book.

Contents

Section Three:
Applying Your Reason

Section Four:
Using Your Intuition to Discover New Possibilities

Acknowledgments

My thanks to the Community Boards of San Francisco, where I was a volunteer for several years on their conflict resolution panels and first became interested in this field.

Introduction

Conflicts are part of everyday living. Everyone has different goals, interests, priorities, agendas, personal styles, you name it—and inevitably these differences lead to conflicts. So what starts off as differences of opinion or different choices escalates, and you have a conflict! Then you have to figure out what to do about it—walk away, sit down and have an extended discussion about the problem, give in to what the other person wants, assert yourself to get your own way, or figure out some kind of compromise. Or maybe there was some way to avoid the differences escalating into a conflict in the first place.

Unfortunately, because of all sorts of factors—personality dynamics, family relationships, power politics, whatever—it is often hard to know what to do. Also, the fear of making the wrong choices, a lack of information, poor communication, analysis paralysis, or other blocks can interfere with resolving a conflict and you might find yourself hanging onto the status quo, unable to move ahead to a better, more satisfying situation, even though you are clearly unsatisfied with the way things are.

Many conflicts can be readily overcome by regarding them as problems to be resolved by identifying the source of the problem and applying the appropriate problem-solving techniques. For example, you might use techniques like creative visualization to examine the reasons for the problem, rational analysis to assess different strategies in your conflict resolution repertoire, brainstorming to come up with alternatives, and mental-control techniques to gain the internal motivation or control to put new solutions into practice.

It may be that you have the resources to solve a conflict yourself, though at times you may need an outside advisor or consultant to assess the situation and suggest conflict remedies. While you may be able to use detachment techniques to separate yourself from the situation and see the conflict more clearly as an outsider, this can be difficult to do when you are embroiled in the battle and emotionally involved. The outsider is already detached and doesn't have the emotional baggage and fears that can stand in the way of seeing or solving the conflict. The outsider can look at the problem dispassionately, recognize the dynamics, and suggest appropriate techniques to come up with effective solutions. However, after reading this book you may be better able to apply these techniques yourself; you may be better able to look at the conflict as an outsider would and recognize the sources of the conflict, think of alternative approaches, decide on the best strategy, and put that into practice yourself.

Applying Conflict Management Techniques to Any Problem

The techniques discussed in this book are designed to help anyone resolve virtually any type of problem, whether inner conflict or conflict between people. The process starts by looking over your major conflicts and determining which ones to deal with first. This involves setting priorities, since you can only work effectively on a few conflicts at a time. Then, once you learn to apply this method, you can apply it to any conflicts you face in the future.

As you'll learn, a key to this approach is to first get your emotions under control, and then look at the reasons for the conflicts and pinpoint the source of tension, so you can come up with the appropriate solutions. For instance, some conflicts are due to circumstances in the situation; others to the personalities of the people involved; still others may point to a recurring behavior pattern or attitude that triggers recurring conflicts.

It is also helpful to understand some of the most common reasons for conflicts, since these models can suggest approaches to use in dealing with your own similar conflicts. Thus, in the book, I have included many real-life examples of conflicts resulting from poor communication and misunderstandings; from different agendas, interests, and values; from political power struggles in a group situation; from wrong assumptions about others' motives and actions; from a lack of empathy with others' needs and wants; and from dealing with difficult people, who require special handling. In addition, since many conflicts are internal ones, where you are torn in different directions in deciding what to do or are held back by fears, a lack of information, or a belief that you can't do something, I've also included techniques for applying this method to those inner conflicts.

I've drawn these real-life examples from workshops, interviews, and some of my own encounters with difficult people and situations. Many of the examples will probably strike some familiar chords.

In the next chapters, I'll outline a basic method for dealing with any type of conflict—an approach I've been using for over two decades, since I started working with conflict and wrote my first book about this, *Resolving Conflict*, published in 1980. Back then, I first started learning about how to resolve conflict as a panelist for Community Boards of San Francisco, a neighborhood conflict resolution group. Then I went to dozens of workshops and seminars on the subject, and gradually my own ideas on dealing with conflict evolved. I began doing seminars and workshops on the subject, and wrote a series of books on dealing with conflict in the workplace: *Work with Me! Resolving Everyday Conflict in Your Organization*; *A Survival Guide for Working With Humans*; *A Survival Guide for Working with Bad Bosses*; and *A Survival Guide to Managing Employees from Hell*. The basic model that I developed back in 1980 has informed all of these later books on resolving conflict—and now this book focuses on the major principles of this model and shows how to apply them in different situations.

Section
One

The Emotional-Rational-Intuitive (E-R-I) Method

Managing Conflict with the E-R-I Model

The possibility for conflict exists everywhere. Conflicts arise out of everyday differences of opinion, disagreements, and the interplay of different ideas, needs, drives, wishes, lifestyles, values, beliefs, interests, and personalities. Yet conflicts are more than just debates or negotiations. They represent an escalation of everyday competition and discussion into an arena of hostile or emotion-provoking encounters that strain personal or interpersonal tranquility, or both.

For example, a bill from your doctor is higher than you expect or think it should be. You go to your doctor to discuss it, and he explains that the amount increase is justified because he spent more time than in a usual office visit. He detected a potential problem and needed to examine you further. Is this a conflict? It's more accurately described as a disagreement or a difference of opinion. But as with any difference of opinion or divergence in personal needs and goals, there is always the potential that a real conflict might develop if the emotions become engaged or hostility is expressed. Say you claim you won't pay the increase because the doctor didn't advise you in advance, and the doctor threatens to no longer treat you as a patient. You then raise complaints about the doctor's previous use of tests you don't think were needed. The result is that at some point, unless you choose to give in and pay whatever the doctor is asking, this discussion turns into a conflict. It becomes a heated verbal combat based on competing or opposing interests, and in some cases, tensions rise even more.

This kind of scenario plays itself out again and again at all levels in human relationships—between spouses, lovers, friends, parents and children, business associates, relatives, neighbors, everybody. And it can occur internally when you face opposing desires and needs that pull you in different directions.

When you don't know how to deal with these situations, the uncomfortable feelings generated by the conflict can be destructive to you and the relationship. The actual outcome of the conflict can be even more unproductive and detrimental. For instance, returning to the doctor example, you might end up paying the increased amount, and feel resentful toward your doctor as a result. This might trigger further hostile encounters, leading eventually to your leaving a doctor who has provided you expert care or to your doctor refusing to further treat you as a patient. In the worst case, the initial discussion might actually escalate from an exchange of heated words to physical violence.

On the other hand, with proper strategy, the potential conflict could be steered into a more favorable resolution. The doctor might agree to defer the extra payment this time or seek to get an extra amount from your insurance carrier, while you agree that you will clarify what you expect on future visits. You might also determine when you need to see this more expensive specialist and when you might obtain routine treatment first from doctors at a local clinic.

Similarly, at work, you might turn a potential conflict into a win-win situation, such as when you and a co-worker are vying for a similar position. Maybe your co-worker is more interested in the title, management duties, and the larger office with a great view that come with the position, while you are more interested in the more challenging technical work you will be doing in the new job. By clarifying what you are each looking for in the new job, you might each be able to get what you want and turn the conflict into a source of opportunity for you both.

In short, with the proper conflict management skills, potential conflicts can be averted or defused—and even turned into a positive source for improved interpersonal relationships and personal growth. The key is not to *avoid* conflict, which is potentially inherent in all social interactions and in all choices we make, but to recognize it and manage it skill-fully to produce the best outcome.

Using the E-R-I Method for Conquering Conflict

An ideal technique for managing conflict is the emotional-rational-intuitive (E-R-I) method of conflict resolution. In essence, this method involves first getting the emotions—yours or the other person's—out of the way. Then, you use your reason and your intuition to make choices about how to react in conflict situations. You base your approach on the circumstances, the personalities, interests, and needs of the people involved, and on your own goals, interests, and needs.

This is a powerful approach because at its heart any serious conflict engages the emotions of its participants. Therefore, one of the first steps in resolving conflict is to defuse the negative emotions generated by the conflict—both your own feelings and that of others. To do so, you need to call on your reason or intuition, because if you react from your own feelings to these already heightened feelings, you will only help to fur-ther raise the emotional tension level instead of defusing it.

Once emotions are defused, you can use your reason or intuition, as appropriate, to figure out possible resolutions acceptable to all involved. But say this is an extremely difficult situation and you can't realistically resolve or defuse emotions now. You might use the rational-intuitive method to decide that the best thing to do now is to delay and walk away so you can obtain more information, as well as cool off the heat of the argument. Then, you can regroup and come back prepared to resolve it. So initially, avoidance can sometimes be just the ticket, rather than trying to work out the problem when you and the other party are still upset and you don't have all the information you need.

Once you learn to understand and assess the situation and make effective choices in the conflict or potential conflict situations you encounter, you will optimize your ability to not only resolve a conflict but even gain from the people with whom you are in conflict. And if a conflict is a barrier to something you want, overcoming it will help you achieve your goal, too.

Here are the basics on how the model works. Subsequent chapters will discuss in more detail how to use each of the three aspects of the model, while the many examples will help you see how the method might be applied in various conflict situations.

How the E-R-I Conflict Management Model Works

The basic way to use the emotional-rational-intuitive approach to managing conflict is to look on any conflict situation as a problem or potential problem to be solved. First, you must get past the emotions involved, so that you can use your reason and intuition to deal with the core problem. Then, you select the appropriate problem-solving techniques from an arsenal of possible strategies for dealing with the conflict. The strategy you select will depend on the stage of the conflict (potential conflict, developing conflict, open conflict), the importance of a particular resolution to you, an assessment of what the other person needs and wants, and the types of emotions released by the conflict.

Once you select the appropriate technique, you then determine the best way to apply it. The optimal choices depend on your ability to assess the situation and the alternatives rationally, your ability to intuit what option is best for the situation, and your ability to put that choice into action.

Whenever you find yourself in a conflict or potential conflict situation, go through a quick "self-assessment" like the one that follows. Depending on your answers, choose the appropriate response. Give yourself time to learn to do this, because at first you will have to think through your reactions. But in time, as you use this approach regularly, the choices will come to you spontaneously. It will be like flashing through all the options in your mind in a moment, then intuitively choosing the ones you want to employ in that situation.

The following chart, which is adapted from my out-of-print book *Resolving Conflict* (originally published in 1990 by New Harbinger Publications, Inc., Oakland, CA), describes the questions to ask and strategies to use. Subsequent chapters describe how and when to use each of these strategies in more detail, so when you are in a conflict situation you can review your options and decide the best ones to choose.

Questions to Ask	Strategies to Use
1. Are emotions causing the conflict or standing in the way of a resolution? If yes: What are these emotions?	**1.** No matter what the emotions, there are techniques to calm feelings, both your own and the other's, so that solutions can be worked out.

• ANGER? If so, whose?
  a. The other person's?
 	
  b. Your own?
	• ANGER
	  a. Techniques to cool down or deflect the anger, such as empathetic listening, letting the other person vent his or her anger, soothing hurt feelings, and correcting misunderstandings.
	  b. Techniques to channel or control your anger, such as short-term venting, deflection, and visualization to release anger.

• MISTRUST? If so, whose?
  a. The other person's?
 	
  b. Your own?
	• MISTRUST
	  a. Techniques to cool down or deflect the anger, such as empathetic listening, letting the other person vent his or her anger, soothing hurt feelings, and correcting misunderstandings.
	  b. Techniques to channel or control your anger, such as short-term venting, deflection, and visualization to release anger.

• FEAR? If so, whose?
  a. The other person's?
  b. Your own?
	• FEAR
	  a. Techniques to reduce fear.
	  b. Techniques to assess the accuracy of this fear or to deal with it openly and productively.

• OTHER EMOTIONS (jealousy, guilt, etc.)? If so, whose?
  a. The other person?
 	
  b. Your own?
	• OTHER EMOTIONS
	
	  a. Techniques to calm the other person.
	  b. Techniques to calm yourself.

2. What are the underlying reasons for the conflict?	**2.** Ways to search for the true needs and wants of both parties.

• WHAT ARE THE OTHER PERSON'S TRUE NEEDS AND WANTS?	• OTHER PERSON'S NEEDS AND WANTS
	  a. Direct communication, asking the person to outline reasons, needs, and wants.
	  b. Intuitive and sensing techniques to pick up the underlying reasons if

- WHAT ARE YOUR OWN TRUE NEEDS AND WANTS?

the person isn't willing to speak or isn't self-aware enough to recognize these underlying needs and wants.

- YOUR NEEDS AND WANTS
  a. Self-examination to determine your real desires and needs if you aren't already clear about them.
  b. Intuitive and sensing techniques to consider your underlying goals.

You Statements (sound accusatory)	I Statements (express feelings, make requests, are solution-oriented)
"You never call me to go somewhere or do something until the last minute."	"When you call me to make plans at the last minute, I'm not always free, although I would like to go with you if I could. I sometimes feel hurt that you wait so long. I would appreciate it if you would call me earlier so we can make arrangements in the future.
"Why do you always interrupt me?"	"When you try to talk to me while I'm talking, I can't really pay attention to what you're trying to say because I'm thinking about something else. I'd really appreciate it if you could wait until I've finished talking, unless it's really important and you feel you have to interrupt right away.
"You don't respect me. You never remember my birthday."	"When you don't remember my birthday I feel like you don't care about me or respect me. I would like to feel that you care."
"You are annoying me with all your questions."	"When you ask me questions while I'm doing something else, I feel distracted and irritate, because I'm not really ready to pay attention to them. I'd appreciate it if you could ask me these questions again at a more convenient time, such as " [you specify when].
"You never do what I want; always what you want."	"When you make a decision for us without asking for my opinion, I feel hurt and I feel that you aren't interested in my ideas. I'd like it if we could discuss these things so we could do what we both want."

What the Person Says	What You Think He or She Means or Feels	What You Might Say to Bring Out the Real Meanings or Feelings
"Do what you want."	"I don't like what you want to do, but I don't feel like you care about what I think. I feel that you are going to do it your way in any event."	"I feel that you may not really want this. What do you *really* want, and can we talk about it?"
"I don't care."	"I do care, but I feel frustrated. You aren't listening to what I am saying."	"But you do seem to be annoyed by what happened, and I'm concerned about how you feel."
"Have it your way."	"I'm too tired to struggle with you anymore. Do what you want, but I don't like it."	"But I'd like to be sure I have your input and agreement, too. What would you like to see happen, so we can both get what we want?"
"Fine" [or any other words of apparent approval that are spoken in a reluctant or angry tone of voice].	"It's not the slightest bit fine, and I'm really very angry with you. I feel like I'm being pushed around."	"But it sounds like it *isn't* fine for you. What do you really feel about this? I'd truly like to know."

Questions to Ask (cont.)

3. Is the conflict due to a misunderstanding? Whose?

  a. The other person's?

  b. Your own?

  c. Both, or Uncertain?

4. Is the conflict due to someone failing to take responsibility for some action, in the past or in the future? Is an agreement to do something needed? Whose responsibility?

  a. The other person's responsibility?

  b. Your responsibility?

Strategies to Use (cont.)

3. Techniques for overcoming misunderstanding through better communication

  a. Techniques to explain and clarify.

  b. Techniques to be open and receptive to the other person's explanations

  c. Combination of techniques to explain and clarify to the other person, and to be open and receptive to the other person's explanations

4. Techniques to determine who is responsible and to gain acceptance for this responsibility.

  a. Techniques to get the other person to acknowledge responsibility and agree to do something.

  b. Techniques to recognize and acknowledge this.

5. What kind of conflict styles would be most suitable to use in this situation?

5. Techniques to assess the available conflict styles, and choosing between them, based on:

- The conflict style you prefer.
- The conflict style you and others feel most comfortable with.
- The conflict styles that would be most effective under the circumstances.

a. Is it possible to reach a win-win solution? If yes:

a. Choose the style of compromise or collaboration, using techniques of negotiation and discussion.

b. Is the conflict worth resolving now? If not:

b. Choose avoidance or delay to postpone dealing with the situation now.

c. Are there power considerations that will affect the outcome? Who is more powerful?

c. If you are more powerful, choose competition or offer to compromise. If the other person is more powerful, choose accommodation or offer to compromise.

6. Do special personality factors come into play?

6. Unfortunately, don't they always?

a. Is the other person a "difficult" person?

a. Special techniques for dealing with difficult people.

b. Do you have difficulty stating your true needs and wants (for example, recognition)?

b. Techniques for expressing your needs and wants effectively.

7. What alternatives and solutions are available?

7. Both parties should be encouraged to make suggestions about possible solutions.

8. How can this conflict/problem be turned into an opportunity?

8. Techniques of brainstorming and creative visualization help achieve positive outcomes.

9. What is the best outcome?

9. Using your rational skills to prioritize possible outcomes will help you create a solution that is the best you can achieve in the circumstances of this particular conflict.

2 Dealing with the Emotions

The first step in handling a conflict is to deal with the emotions, either your own or someone else's. Whether expressed outwardly or inwardly, these bubble up and create tension that prevents handling the conflict. Even if not expressed directly, such as in angry words or an explosion of rage, emotions can fester inwardly and lead to resentment, sabotage, avoidance strategies, and other negative behaviors that interfere with relationships or productivity on the job.

Even a passing torrent of emotions, if not dealt with and worked through, can poison what had been a good relationship. For example, when Sue had a leak in a newly built room in her basement, the builder Sam initially proposed further construction to put in a drain. But when she asked another builder she met for a quote, just for a point of comparison, the second builder suggested she first find out the source of the leak. So she called Sam to ask him to wait before starting the new project until she could determine what caused the leak.

Before then, she had had a good relationship with Sam, who had done numerous projects for her, but as soon as she mentioned finding out what happened, Sam exploded, yelling at her, "I know what you are going to do! You'll have people come in! They'll lie! You're going to pin it all on me!" Then he slammed down the phone.

The result was that Sue was literally afraid to even communicate with Sam anymore and brought in a lawyer to represent her. In time, Sam's temper cooled down, and he eventually agreed to fix the leak, saying he wanted to do the right thing. Yet in the language of legal agreements, he didn't acknowledge responsibility and never apologized for his angry outburst, leaving a residue of distrust and suspicion, so Sue never did call on him for future projects. If Sam had managed his anger in the first place, he and Sue might have more amicably worked out a resolution for fixing the leak, and she would have continued to look to him for future projects.

Thus, a first step in any conflict is to either 1) get rid of the negative emotions, or 2) control or channel them in essence, to *tame* any negative emotions you or anyone else still have.

The negative emotions include feelings of anger, hatred, resentment, mistrust, fear, jealousy, and envy. These arise for various reasons and often seem justified, such as when you are angry because you feel betrayed, disrespected, taken advantage of, ignored, or subjected to bureaucratic snafus and slow-downs.

But justified or not, you'll get further in solving the conflict if you overcome your negative feelings or at least control how you express them. In fact, there are times when you can benefit from showing your anger, such as if you are an irate customer seeking management help in correcting a problem. But if you temper your rage and release it in a controlled way, like an actor expressing anger on a stage, you will be taken more seriously and evoke efforts to placate you. If you explode like a maniac, you'll be defined as a nut case who needs to be calmed down and ejected, not someone with a problem that needs to be resolved.

I'll deal in more detail with handling some of the major negative feelings—anger, mistrust, and fear—in Chapters 5 and 6. But here I want to briefly describe what to do to begin to get a handle on any negative emotion.

When Someone Else Is Upset

First, if it's someone else's negative emotion, there are several strategies: listening calmly, apologizing, and walking away (delaying). Let's examine each of these options.

Learning to Listen Calmly

One strategy for dealing with others' emotions is to simply listen and let them vent. This is a technique I first learned at Community Board meetings, where we heard mostly neighbors' disputes, and some involving friends and family. Commonly, when someone else yells at you or makes angry accusations, often untrue ones, your first reaction will be to respond in kind by yelling back at the person or countering with your own accusations. Or perhaps you may want to fight back with reasonable explanations, excuses, or arguments, showing why the other person is wrong or has misjudged you, or explaining away what happened. Or possibly you may want to acknowledge a problem but make promises for the future.

However, as long as the other person is still angry, upset, fearful, or otherwise caught up in the emotions of the moment, your response, whatever it is, is not likely to be effective. The person probably is so involved in the emotional moment that he or she is not able to absorb anything else. So any effort you make at this point is like putting tinder on a raging fire; you only increase the blaze or keep it going. For example, if you yell back, the person is apt to yell even louder; if you throw out a reason, however good it may be, the person is likely to reject it out of hand and keep going.

Thus, a better strategy is to simply listen respectfully, just to show you are hearing and understanding, not necessarily that you agree with what's being said. Your lack of agreement can come later. But for now, you want to just listen, and to show you are listening, you should occasionally nod or say noncommittal words of understanding, such as "Uhhmmm . . . hummm" or "Yes."

The process is like letting a kettle blow off steam, so it cools down. It's an approach that cops have learned to use effectively. They stand there stoically while someone who's upset lets it all hang out, such as the motorist angry at being stopped or the suspect furious about being handcuffed. After a time, the person finishes with their emotional rampage and calms down, sometimes because the emotional fury is released, sometimes out of pure exhaustion.

Then, once the person seems calmer, you can share your own point of view—or perhaps ask the person if you can set up another time to have this discussion, when you are both calm and ready for it.

At Community Boards, the way we handled this process was to have the conflicting parties, "the disputants," sit initially facing us. Then, in turn, we would ask each party to say whatever he or she wanted about the dispute, while the other person just listened quietly without saying anything. And if the other person did try to respond back, we would simply say: "You'll have a chance to respond later," and then the first party would continue. After a few minutes of this, we would switch their roles, and the other person would get to tell his or her side of the story, and share his or her own gripes.

The process is called "venting," like letting each heated kettle release its steam. The participants then could calmly share their views about the problem. And if there were still strong feelings at the next stage, people could take some more time venting to get rid of those last bits of hot steam.

Similarly, you can often do the same thing. Just let the person rant and rave or otherwise get his or her feelings out. It's an approach that usually works to defuse the situation, though in some cases, you may need to either leave the theater of conflict for awhile or bring in a third neutral party to do your listening for you. This is much like what a mediator does in dealing with a conflict—he or she lets each party vent to get their emotions out in the open and calm them down, before going onto the next stage of the mediation. However, if violence is threatened, you may want to walk away. However, it's best to back off respectfully, so you don't enrage the person even more or make yourself vulnerable when you do turn away.

Showing That You're Sorry

Another approach for deflecting others' emotions, if appropriate, is to sincerely apologize for something you may have done wrong or show the person you are truly sorry for whatever happened (even if you yourself have nothing to apologize for). Or there may be other gestures or actions you can take to show submission or deference to the other person, so he or she feels less defensive and feels a boost to his or her self-esteem.

Such actions can be very calming, like applying salve to an open wound. It cools it down and helps it start to heal—which is what you want in human relationships, too.

Walking Away or Delaying

If just listening isn't working and apologizing or showing submission isn't an appropriate or effective strategy—or if you feel threatened by someone who is angry—another major strategy is to walk away or ask to delay the encounter and then leave.

For example, some person you unintentionally cut off in a parking lot is now yelling and screaming at you. It may be better to just back off rather than trying to fight it. People have gotten seriously injured or even killed when they have tried to stand up to someone who is in the middle of a rage over some perceived wrong or slight. There's no sense trying to explain if someone isn't going to be receptive to whatever you are saying.

When *You* Are the One Who's Upset

Certainly, it's easier to deal with someone else's emotional discharge when you are calm yourself. But what if you are upset, whether or not the other person is upset. In this situation, you need to deal with releasing your own emotions or getting them under control. Here are some ways to do that.

Calming Yourself Down

If you can, calm yourself down on the spot! Then, if the other person is calm or you can subsequently calm the other person down, you can deal with resolving the conflict right then and there. There are a number of techniques presented here that you can use to calm yourself down, many of which are adapted from my previous book, *The Empowered Mind: How to Harness the Creative Force Within You* (New York: iUniverse, 2006; originally Prentice Hall, 1994).

Notice When You Are Feeling Angry or Upset

While you can clearly tell that you are angry when you outwardly express your feelings by screaming, yelling, or sobbing, you can also pick up *inner* mental or physical signs that you are growing angry or upset. If you can notice them before you explode openly, you can short-circuit the process and decide if you *want* to express your anger—and *how*. In fact, this is one approach used by groups trying to help men overcome their violence against women. They guide them to become aware of the signs of their anger so they can hold themselves back from hitting their wives or girlfriends, say by going for a walk or hitting a pillow in another room. Such signs include things like feelings of rising tension, a tightening in the muscles, an increase in the speed, intensity, and repetition of self-talk focused on the incident causing the anger, and anything else which you associate with anger.

Stop or Hold Back Your Feelings of Anger or Upset When You Feel the Signs

Once you experience the signs of anger or upset coming on, you can stop yourself from expressing it or you can channel it into another form of expression in order to avoid expressing it inappropriately or destructively.

Say you feel your boss or co-worker is tearing you down for something that wasn't your fault, or for which you have a good reason. Or say you have just learned that a friend has said or done something you consider a betrayal. You feel ready to blow and sound off. But rather than blast out your feelings, which might lose you your job or undermine a long friendship, you can hold yourself back and control how and when you express your feelings. The idea is not to be a wimp or punching bag who just takes it, but to manage how you express your feelings so you express them wisely. For example, your anger with your boss might lead to a reasoned discussion of the problems that are bothering you, resulting in a successful resolution; your anger with a friend you believe betrayed you, if confirmed, can lead to a planned strategic break where you protect your own interests, rather than an immediate angry eruption leading to a disruptive, traumatic break.

Some ways to stop, deflect, and channel those feelings include:

Ask for or take some time out. This way you can get away from the situation or person causing you to feel a growing anger or upset. Taking time out can also give you time to calm down, get your feelings under control, and if appropriate, check out your assumptions or the information you have been given that is causing you to feel angry, because you could be wrong. For instance, maybe the friend you are angry at didn't betray you and someone else is spreading rumors to hurt you or break-up a powerful alliance. This time-out can also be combined with a visualization technique which helps you to let go of and release or redirect your anger or upset feelings in a more positive way.

Use calming self-talk to calm yourself down. Telling yourself calming things helps direct your attention away from what is bothering you and counters the feelings inside you that are contributing to your anger. Using self-talk can also short-circuit any immediate impulse you have to lash out verbally or physically and can help you feel more detached and less emotional about the situation. For example, you might tell yourself things like: "Calm down. Relax. This problem isn't so important . . . You don't have to react now . . . Don't take this personally . . . Don't let this bother you." You can also use self-talk to encourage personal projection or detachment to remove yourself from an upsetting situation.

Use personal projection or detachment to remove yourself from the situation. In this case, you simply imagine yourself not there. You mentally go away or experience yourself stepping out of yourself and watching yourself, so you are no longer emotionally affected by the situation you are in. The process is a kind of disassociation, which people sometimes do when they experience great trauma or stress they can't deal with. To protect their psyche they disconnect from whatever they are experiencing, so they feel it happened to someone else. They may not be aware of this process until they reconnect the pieces they have disconnected from later. However, in this case, you are fully aware of and in charge of the process, so you become like an observer and film director, rather than an actor, in your own film. You can use self-talk to guide you into this state or simply imagine yourself somewhere else.

Remind yourself not to take it personally. Telling yourself "Don't take it personally" is a good way to short-circuit the common reaction to respond defensively to a situation in which you feel someone has mistreated, disrespected, or otherwise wronged you. Often such actions are due to the person's own problems, and you are just a handy scapegoat, such as when a boss, angered by a fight with her husband, snaps at her employees at work and starts finding fault with everything. In a situation like this, a good way to reduce your defensiveness and readiness to respond in anger is to tell yourself repeatedly not to take it personally. For example, tell yourself something like: "It isn't me . . . She (or he) is just angry and is taking it out on me." By telling yourself it's not a personal attack on you, you can help to distance yourself from the situation, so you yourself feel less upset and angry. Then, if you just listen without expressing anger, the other person will calm down and may even be ready to share what is going on, and the problem will resolve itself, whereas an angry reaction on your part would only have increased the tension.

Use a visualization to let go of or transform your anger or feelings of upset. Although most visualizations can take some time, a few can be done quickly during the situation causing you to feel angry or upset. Here are some quick visualizations you can use to overcome your negative feelings. (You can use longer visualizations when you are confronting an ongoing difficult situation and can take some private time to unwind and transform a negative situation into a positive time.) Use these quick-time techniques for more spur-of-the-moment situations. Use whichever ones feel most comfortable to you, combine them together, or create your own.

• *Release the anger or other negative emotion by grounding it out.* As you feel anger or another negative emotion rising within you, imagine that it is coming into you like a beam of negative energy from the person or situation that is upsetting you. Then, imagine this energy moving downward within you and dispersing harmlessly into the ground.

• *Stop the build-up of anger or negative emotion by blocking it out.* Visualize a wall of white light or a bubble or dome of protection around you which is a barrier between you and the situation or person causing you to feel distressed. Then, imagine that whatever the person is saying or whatever events are bothering you are being deflected off this barrier, while you are safe, isolated, and protected inside.

• *Release the anger or other negative emotion by projecting it out and eliminating it.* To release your negative feelings, visualize a large screen in front of you. Then, imagine you are sending out the anger or other negative emotions like a laser beam and projecting it onto the screen. Next, imagine you are holding a ray-gun and shooting at those feelings. Each time you zap them, you experience the anger releasing and draining away.

• *Release the anger by cutting the person who makes you angry down to size.* This technique is especially suitable if you are dealing with someone who is more powerful than you (as on the job) or if this person has acquired a strong power over you emotionally (such as an ex-significant other). To deal with this situation on-the-spot, you might imagine something like this: As this person is shouting at you, imagine him or her growing smaller and smaller right before your eyes. But don't smile while you are doing this, which might further anger the person. When the tirade is over, you can calmly try to find out what is bothering the person.

If you have more time to deal with the issue, you might take some private time to do a visualization like the following. Start the visualization by seeing yourself talking to this person. See him or her doing whatever makes you angry. Then, as you talk, notice this person is shrinking in size and his or her voice is becoming fainter and fainter. Meanwhile, you are feeling stronger and stronger and more powerful, while this person is becoming less and less powerful and important in your life. Then, you can say goodbye and leave this tiny person, feeling very powerful yourself. Or—if you feel especially angry at this person imagine him or her as small as a bug that you squash under your foot.

- *Release the anger by taking some mental revenge.* If you really feel angry, taking some mental revenge might help release your feelings, though if you find that thinking such thoughts makes you even more angry and upset, then this isn't a good technique for you. But if you find thinking vengeful thoughts works as a helpful catharsis, by all means use this technique to imagine yourself or a representative taking some action to appropriately punish the person who has wronged you. Then, as if you were at a film, just observe what happens on your mental screen. And let yourself enjoy the "film," in which you express your revenge.

Have the attitude of learning or profiting from the experience.
Although you might use this approach later to transform a bad experience into something with some benefit, because you learn from or can profit from it, it can also help you release your feelings of anger or upset. Why? Because knowing the situation can later be used for your own benefit can help you feel better about the situation now. It can help you detach and see the situation in a more neutral way, because you realize you can transform it into a positive. To use this technique, just tell yourself: "I can learn from or profit from this experience later. So don't be so upset now."

For a more long-term fix, ask yourself: "What can I learn from this situation which I can use in the future?" or "How can I turn this situation into something from which I can profit?" Or ask yourself these questions later, in a quiet, private space. By reminding yourself that every experience has this potential and knowing that you can take some time now or in the future to imagine how these possibilities might be realized, you can help to release your emotional upset and anger about something in the here and now.

Creating and using a calming trigger. This is a technique that works if you have already taken the time to create a "trigger" to calm yourself down. The way to create this trigger is to associate a gesture, such as snapping your fingers or touching your ear, with a relaxation response, such as feeling very calm and peaceful. Repeat the gesture and the response over and over, until you have conditioned this response. Later, when you feel you are becoming angry or upset, use can use this gesture to evoke your relaxation response.

Remove Yourself from the Anger-Provoking or Upsetting Situation or Person

If you are not able to calm yourself down on the spot, remove yourself from the situation or person, so you can come back later when you are calmed down. This way rather than just trying to mentally detach, you physically detach, which can help you detach mentally and emotionally as well. There are a few ways to do this, sometimes in combination:

- Excuse yourself, saying "I'm not feeling well right now," and just walk away.

- Do something you like to do that makes you feel relaxed and puts you in a good mood, such as going to a movie, going sailing, talking a walk around a park, going to visit a friend, going out for dinner, throwing a ball around, participating in a favorite hobby or sport—whatever you like doing.

- Do something that helps you release your feelings of anger or frustration, such as going to the gym and pumping iron or hitting a boxing bag. Sometimes eating something you like will help—but be careful here not to create a weight problem for yourself by turning to eating whenever you are upset; if this is the case, find another form of release.

- Ask the person for some time out, so you can deal with the situation later.

- Use your time away from the situation to get additional information that can help you deal with the problem.

- If the other person is already calm, you might share your feelings of mistrust, fear, or anger, in the hopes that this might clear the air. The other person may try to soothe your hurt or angry feelings. (But don't try to do this if the other person is also angry and upset; then he or she may throw back what you have shared like a weapon, to attack you when you have made yourself more vulnerable by sharing your feelings.)

In sum, there are many ways you can deal with the negative emotions unleashed by a conflict. Whatever way you choose, the first step in resolving a conflict is to eliminate or control these feelings. You can then turn to your reason and intuition, which can help you resolve the problem.

3

Using Your Reason

Once the emotions are out of the way, the next step in dealing with a conflict is using your reason to understand the basis for the conflict, including unstated positions and agendas. Then, using your reason to understand the different conflict resolution styles, you can choose which one or combination of styles would be most appropriate for dealing with this particular conflict. I'll discuss these topics more extensively in Section Three. Here I want to introduce the basic components of the reason component of the E-R-I conflict resolution model.

What Is Causing the Conflict?

Sometimes it's very clear what a conflict is about. You want to do one thing; your friend or significant other wants to do another. Your boss wants you to work extra hours over the holidays, and is even willing to pay you more, but you just want to chill out with your friends and loved ones.

But at other times, the conflict is ostensibly about one thing, when in fact there are hidden or unexpressed motivations fueling the conflict. In such a situation, your proposed solution for the conflict won't work very well, because the conflict is really about something else. For example, a mother objects to her son's choice of a mate, claiming she is too old, since she is ten years older than he is. But in fact the real reasons for the mother's objections are 1) that the two are of different religions, and 2) that her son is being drawn into the woman's network in the art world, when the mother wants him to be a lawyer or doctor. So the argument goes round and round about the mother's objections that the girl isn't good enough for him and he should find someone his own age. But the argument is really a cover for her own agenda, which she doesn't want to express, since outwardly she claims she wants to support her son's career choices.

Likewise at work, one co-worker may continually be finding fault with another's contributions, finding reasons why the work doesn't measure up. But in fact, the co-worker is finding fault because she doesn't want her associate gaining recognition and getting a promotion; it's much more comforting to keep the co-worker in her place, so she will give up her long-terms goals and aspirations.

This is where your reason comes in—as you seek to puzzle out exactly what's really going on. Sometimes your intuition can help you when you sense that something isn't exactly right and leads you to delve deeper. But then your reason—your analytical thinking process—is what can help you think about different possibilities and different likely scenarios. With the help of your intuition, you can determine what fits in this particular situation.

And naturally, your reason can help you in recognizing and assessing which of the common reasons for a conflict are most applicable in this case. Some of the major reasons to consider are these:

1. **Different Needs, Interests, or Values**. You like one thing; the other person prefers something else. While with different interests this can sometimes lend itself to a fairly easy solution—such as you do that and I'll do this, and we'll do something else together or let's both do this first and then we'll both do that—when you have different needs or values that can be trickier. That's because it may not be so easy for one person to compromise, such as when one person is a stickler for healthy foods or strict vegan cooking, and the person's partner just loves hamburgers and fries. Or say you work in a sales department where the ideal is making the sale, and your supervisor wants you to cut corners and not be particularly forthright about why the more expensive model may not be needed by the prospective clients. But you feel that approach is unethical, and you insist on being forthright, even if it means losing the sale.

One of the keys to resolving a conflict can be knowing the other person's real needs, interests, and fears, so you can take these into consideration in coming up with a resolution that works for you both. Then, too, recognizing and considering the importance of a particular issue to you and others can be a factor in helping you achieve a mutually satisfying resolution.

2. **Poor Communication**. This is a big one. Read any of the popular advice columns and you'll find that poor communication is at the root of many misunderstandings. People often don't say what they mean or mean what they say. Information doesn't get communicated clearly or at all. Or you think that you conveyed a message, but the other person doesn't get it—and doesn't want to let you know he or she didn't get it; so you think he or she got it and act accordingly. (Chapter 8 is devoted to this topic.)

Some of the basics to be discussed include these keys for improved communication:

- Be aware of nonverbal signals.

- Share real thoughts and feelings.

- Express feelings without threat, such as by being calm and non-judgmental and using "I statements," rather than critical-sounding "you statements."

- Seek clarity and correct what is unclear or wrong by clarifying what is unclear, correcting misunderstandings, and overcoming hidden and wrong assumptions.

- Learn to listen well by being attentive, reflecting back that you understand, asking about what you don't, as well as by showing respect, having empathy, and listening without judgment.

- Focus on the issues, so you don't get sidetracked onto irrelevant or less important topics.

3. **Lack of Information or Wrong Assumptions.** Sometimes this is due to poor communication or leads to it. Here the problem is you or the other person doesn't have the necessary information or understanding. This leads to confusion and contributes to conflict. Or you or the other person are acting on wrong assumptions—frequently the source of humor in a romantic comedy, where the hero or heroine leaps to wrong conclusions about someone's actions or intentions. This may

be very funny in a movie or play, but it's not so funny when wrong assumptions lead to wrong actions producing real conflict in real life.

4. **Problems Around Power, Control, and Responsibility.** Call it "office politics" or "personal politics"—but issues of who's in charge, what followers are supposed to do, and who's responsible or not responsible for what frequently lead to conflict, too. For example, a subordinate gets conflicting instructions from two different bosses; a person who doesn't have the formal authority steps up to the plate when someone else isn't around to take responsibility; several underlings vie for power when there seems to be a vacuum at the top; and someone jealous about someone else exercising too much power seeks to cut that person down to size. The possibilities for conflict in situations of this kind can read like a thriller—and sometimes they become just that.

5. **Difficult People and Personality Clashes**. Here you just have trouble getting along with someone who's got a hard-to-get-along-with personality—or maybe it's just because of the way your personalities mesh together that creates a clash. Yet you have to learn to work together or at least coexist in a family or a sometimes rocky friendship. In fact, dealing with difficult people is one of the most popular topics in workshops on difficult workplace relationships—from how to deal with the steamroller or backstabber to the shy retiring violet or office sloth. (You'll find out how to deal with difficult people in Chapter 12.)

6. **Lack of Trust.** Another big trigger for conflict is lack of trust by either party. A key consideration here is whether the mistrust is justified. Sometimes it is, but sometimes it is based on false information or assumptions; so getting clarification can help to dispel this mistrust. On the other hand, if you don't trust someone, you may fear to get the issue out in the open—and likewise, a person who distrusts you may fear an open discussion as well. So what to do?

Knowing the Appropriate Strategies to Use

Once you have an understanding of the issues, you can better determine what strategy to apply in a particular situation. Some considerations to help you decide include the following:

• Knowing about the five conflict styles and considering which ones are best to apply in what situations

- Recognizing your own personal style preferences and that of others in the conflict
- Considering the importance of the issue to you and the other person
- Taking into account your relationship with other the person, and in particular, the power balance between the two of you
- Weighing the costs and benefits of taking a particular action
- Considering how well the solution addresses the reasons for the conflict

Here's how to use these various factors in choosing a strategy.

Using the Five Conflict Styles and Choosing Which Ones to Apply When

Consider the five conflict styles like having a repertoire of conflict-resolving techniques. Certain ones may be more appropriate under certain conditions, and you may feel more comfortable using certain styles for most conflicts. But by knowing about these different approaches and their uses, you can better choose which one to use in a particular situation.

You'll see a chart on the following page illustrating the five conflict styles, based on the grid originally developed by Kenneth W. Thomas and Ralph H. Kilmann in 1972 as the Thomas-Kilmann Conflict Mode Instrument. The five styles were developed using a grid based on how assertive you are in satisfying your own concerns and how cooperative you are in satisfying the other person's concerns. If you are assertive without being concerned about the other person's concerns, you are being "confrontational" or "competitive," where you seek to get what you want in a forceful way. If you are assertive but take the other person's concerns into account, you are working together towards a "collaborative" resolution. If you are not assertive and focused on satisfying the other person, you are being "accommodating." If you are neither assertive nor dealing with the other person's concerns, you are "avoiding" the issue. And finally, if you are each giving and taking a little, you are being "compromising."

Knowing When to Use Different Styles

So when should you use different styles? Here's a brief summary. (You'll see a more extended discussion about this in Chapter 9.)

Conflict Handling Styles Matrix

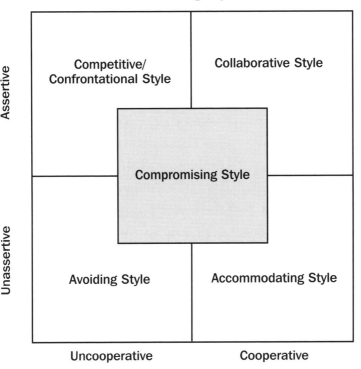

Competitive/Confrontational Style

- Issue important or big stake in outcome.
- Have power and authority.
- No other options; nothing to lose.
- Quick decision needed; emergency situation.
- At an impasse; can't get group agreement.
- Unpopular decision needed and you have the power to make it.

Avoiding Style

- Issue unimportant or little stake in outcome.
- Lack power to resolve situation well or at all.
- Can't win or low chance of winning.
- Want to delay to get information or help.

- Want to cool down tensions.
- Danger of worse conflict if it becomes open.
- Others can or will resolve the matter better.

Accommodating Style

- Issue unimportant, don't care about outcome.
- Have little power, no or low chance of winning.
- Issue and outcome more important to others.
- Want to keep peace; harmony with others important.
- Good relationship more important than issue.
- You are wrong, the other person is right.
- Other person might learn from situation though wrong.

Collaborative Style

- Issue important to both.
- Similar power or willing to put aside power differences.
- Have a close, continuing, interdependent relationship.
- Have time and willing to spend time and effort.
- Both able to discuss and listen.

Compromising Style

- Have different goals, and goals not too important.
- Have similar power.
- Want resolution quickly; temporary resolution okay.
- Provides short-term gain.
- A fallback position when collaboration or competition don't work.
- Compromise is better than nothing.

Taking into Consideration Your Own Style and That of Others

While the above list of styles and when to use them provides a good framework for deciding what to do when, you must also consider your own style preferences and that of others in the conflict, and modify your choices accordingly. For example, the compromising approach may be a good choice if you want a quick solution. Yet if you or the other party would feel more comfortable taking some extra time to discuss the issue in more depth, it may be better to be more collaborative. It will be longer and messier to achieve the resolution, but it may be more enduring since you will have more buy-in from all parties, because you all have invested more effort in coming up with a resolution.

In considering your own and others' styles, some of the factors to consider are these:

- What is your and the other person's primary style?
- What is your and the other person's secondary style?
- What styles do you or other person use or prefer the most or least?
- What success have you had in using different styles to resolve a conflict?
- When have you been most and least successful?

The answers you have given to the above questions will help you in deciding what approach to use now and in the future.

Other Considerations

Finally, here are some other considerations in deciding which approach to use in resolving a conflict:

1. **The importance of the issue to you and the other person.** This factor can help you decide if this is something you really want to stand up for and fight for or not—and if the other person does. Consider this the "choosing-your-battles" principle. If something's really important to you, then perhaps you should take a more confrontational, in-your-face competitive approach, though if *everything* is really important to you, maybe you're being overly confrontational and it's time to back down. You must learn to figure out what's less important. This is particularly useful if you determine that the issue is especially important to the other person, because it could lead to a head-on collision. Such kinds of bargains are commonly made in politics, where one person makes a concession on something of lesser importance to get something of greater importance. This is mirrored by the politician on the other side who gives different values to these issues, so what is more important to one is of lesser importance to the other and vice versa. The

same kind of exchange, based on valuing different issues differently, can work in everyday personal and work relationships, too.

2. **Your relationship with the other person and the power balance between you.** Here's where considerations of the strength of your personal relationship and who's got the power come into play. For example, if you have a very strong bond with someone, sometimes appealing to friendship or a long-term relationship can help to bring that person to the table to work out a resolution, because they don't want to break that bond. On the other hand, if you don't know someone very well, a more neutral approach may be in order. As for the power balance—if you have less power, it's generally not good to take a more confrontational or competitive approach since you are more apt to lose in a power struggle. If you've got more power or have an equal amount of power, then you can be more assertive where an issue is more important to you.

3. **The costs and benefits of taking a particular action**. Still another way of assessing what to do in a conflict is to examine the costs and benefits of different options. Consider what you will lose, what you will gain, what you risk to get what you want, and ask, is it worth it? For example, say you are engaged in an ongoing struggle with someone you live with, a little like a war with many battles. You have fights about whether the windows should be opened or closed, whether the room is too cold or too hot, and about who is going to do what chore when. You might consider whether winning a particular battle is worth fighting for; it may be better to give in on something that is less important to you and to use that as a bargaining chip to get something that's more important. To this end, you might even give each issue of conflict a value, so you can assess what it will cost you to take action to win the result versus the benefit you might gain in winning it. Then, you can better focus your efforts on winning the most worthy battles and giving in on the others.

4. **How well the solution addresses the reasons for the conflict**. Finally, consider the effectiveness of a particular solution in addressing the reason the conflict occurred. Consider if this is a short-term or temporary fix versus a long-term, permanent resolution. Consider whether the solution resolves the apparent conflict or the underlying issues that have led to the conflict. In some cases, the short-term temporary fix

that deals with the outward conflict is just what you need to buy some peace for awhile. But for a more final resolution, you need a more permanent choice that deals with the underlying reasons for the conflict. And sometimes there is no right answer—just different choices, depending on what you and the other party prefer to do at the time.

✦　✦　✦　✦　✦

In sum, by understanding the reasons for a conflict and the different strategies for dealing with a conflict, you can better choose which strategies are most appropriate for dealing with a particular conflict. Then your intuition can help in both making that choice and implementing it to solve that conflict.

Working with Your Intuition

Once you have a general understanding of the conflict and the major strategies and factors to take into consideration, the final step in the process is working with your intuition to come up with alternatives and decide the best choice for you. It may seem like this is an extended process; however, once you have developed an understanding about the different processes to use in assessing a conflict and when to apply them, your intuition literally snaps into place. The previous stages—dealing with your emotions and understanding and assessing the problem—are collapsed, so you can quickly access your intuition to guide you in knowing what to do. All the phases seem to blend together and you feel a strong sense of knowing what to do, so you can quickly make a decision and act.

The basic ways to work with your intuition, discussed further in Section Four, include:

- Brainstorming and creative problem solving to come up with ideas and alternatives for what to do

- Visualization and mental imaging to see yourself implementing different conflict resolution strategies and assessing the results

- Using your gut feelings, combined with your awareness of what's going on, to decide what to do and give you the confidence to resolutely act

Brainstorming and Creative Problem-Solving

Brainstorming is frequently used in companies and group meetings to come up with ideas for planning, such as making suggestions for events and programs for an organization or creating marketing and promotional campaigns. It also makes an excellent way to come up with ideas for creative conflict resolution in your personal life. You let your intuitive mind go, unrestrained by your logical mind, to think of whatever ideas come to mind. Then later you can decide which are feasible and which you really want to put into place to act on.

There are a number of ways to release or communicate with this creative part of your mind, discussed in more length in Section Four. Here I'll just mention some of these techniques briefly. First get in a relaxed, receptive state of mind, and then you can:

Call on your inner expert for alternatives and solutions. This inner expert can take varying forms, such as a revered teacher, guardian spirit or angel, computer guru, a sympathetic friend who just wants to help. But whatever type of guide you use, you speak to that expert as if you are talking with another person and ask for advice. Then, without trying to control the conversation, you simply listen to what your guide has to say. (It may be that your "guide" is in fact your inner thinking responding to a question you put to it, but anthropomorphizing the process helps to make it more vivid and meaningful.) Then decide on the advice that seems most helpful and put that into practice. You might find a quiet place to do this when you are just starting out, since this will help you focus and receive insights, but after awhile, this is a technique you can do anywhere and anytime. Just call on your inner expert or guide mentally wherever you are, and listen for what your expert or guide has to say.

Take a mental journey for ideas and choices. This is a somewhat more elaborate and intense form of calling on your inner expert or guide. But instead of quickly inviting your expert or guide into your mind to help you, you take an extended mental journey to seek information either from an expert or guide or from any other source that may have knowledge to share with you. For instance, you might imagine yourself going up a mountain to visit a wise man in a cabin with answers for you; you might visualize yourself going to the ocean or a waterfall, where you see ideas bubbling up in the water; you might go into your workshop where you turn on your computer and see a solution appearing on the screen, and so on. Wherever you go for insight, the process is similar. You visualize yourself going on a journey somewhere, which helps to take you deep into your creative imagination; then you ask a question, open yourself to be receptive to the answer, and then you hear the answer spoken to you or you see it appear before you.

Look within. Still another approach to tap into your intuitive powers is to use a meditative approach to look within yourself. Rather than calling on an inner expert or taking a journey to find ideas on what to do, you get in a quiet meditative state and ask yourself a series of questions about the reasons for the conflict and what you really want for yourself. The advantage of this meditative state is that it makes you very receptive; when you ask questions, if you just wait, you will hear or see the answer pop into your mind with suggestions on what to do. Later you can evaluate the different options, but consider them to be coming from the wisdom of your inner creative self. Some questions to ask include, but are not limited to: "What do I really want to do about this problem?" "What is holding me back from getting that?" "Should I really work on resolving this conflict, or should I let it go and move on?" "How can I turn this bad experience into a positive outcome?" "What can I learn from what happened?"

Using Visualization to Choose a Conflict Resolution Style

Another way to apply your intuitive abilities is to use visualization to choose among the different conflict resolution styles and imagine how to apply them in a particular situation. To do this, you first need to know what the different conflict styles are and the types of situations where they are most applicable (using your reason to get to this point). Then, you use a visualization to project yourself into the problem situation and imagine different outcomes using different conflict approaches. Finally, you choose among them to decide which is best. It's a method I've used in many workshops on resolving conflict, and at the end of the process, you have a clear vision of what you are going to do next.

The basic steps of the process are these:

1. **Visualize a stage or screen in theater.** See yourself as a director seated alone in the audience where you are directing a theatrical play on stage or a film that is running on the screen.

2. **Watch a conflict situation play out on the screen.** You can run through any conflict you have experienced in your work or personal life which you want to resolve.

3. **Imagine different approaches and outcomes.** To do this, see yourself appearing on the screen where the conflict situation is playing out; then, in turn, try out each of the conflict resolution approaches—confrontation or competition, accommodation, avoidance, collaboration, and compromise—and see what happens. If you are already on screen, embroiled in the conflict, imagine that you are your higher self observing yourself interacting on the stage or screen. Then, tell yourself to apply one of the conflict styles and see what you do.

4. **Choose among the approaches; decide what to do.** Now reflect back on the different scenarios you observed and decide which one worked the best. If there's a second approach that's a strong contender, consider this your back-up plan or plan B. If you find any barriers to carrying out your preferred approach, try that.

5. **See the problem resolved and feel good.** Now in your mind's eye, let the resolution you have chosen play itself out and feel confident and reassured that you have chosen wisely. This doesn't meant that this approach will necessarily work exactly as you envision it, since all sorts of real-world factors can intervene to shape your resolution. For example, your boss can go thumbs down on your new idea, saying it's too expensive. But then your effective presentation of one idea can help to prepare the way so your boss is even more receptive when you bring him another idea. Or maybe Aunt Martha will nix your idea of joining your family on a weekend jaunt, where you can all sit down and have a family gathering to work out an area of disagreement. But at least you might compliment yourself for getting Aunt Martha to recognize there is an ongoing problem, so she will be more receptive to having this family discussion in the future.

6. **Observe the film credits listing you as the film ends.** Finally, give yourself some well-deserved credit for using the creative process to come up with positive ways to resolve the conflict. Whether your approach is actually the one that achieves a resolution or whether it helps to show that you have to let the problem go and walk away, you still deserve to pat yourself on the back and see yourself rewarded.

Using Your Gut Feelings or Sense of Knowing to Decide What to Do

A final tool in your arsenal is your sense of knowing, which sometimes manifests as a "gut feeling" that this is what to do, though it can come to you as a clear vision, a voice speaking to you, or just a sense of certainty about what to do. However, it's very important to couple your sense of knowing—your gut feeling—with information or rational awareness; otherwise you may be led astray by misinformation or biases that could trigger a strong feeling. Thus, it can be helpful to check out how accurately your gut feeling has worked in the past. If it has mostly been accurate, you can continue to trust it. Otherwise, take some time to look at when your feelings have led you astray to determine what might be triggering these wrong feelings.

For example, one woman often confused her own misplaced expectations of what someone should do for a gut level feeling that she didn't trust the person. But in fact, she wasn't communicating what she wanted very well and was continually changing her mind about what she wanted, because she was new to the field and uncertain about what to do. For example, when one man said he would do a proposed budget for a project on spec but was waiting for an agreement from her, she never provided that agreement and felt he was dishonest in offering to do the budget. Moreover, she kept changing the plans for the project, which would result in changes for the budget as well. She didn't realize he was waiting for her to act first, and she didn't follow-up with him to confirm what he expected in order to do the budget.

But once you do have a clear awareness about something and have to make a choice, looking to your gut feelings, inner vision, inner voice, or sense of knowing can be a good way to make that decision. It can also help you make a decision quickly and decisively.

Section One Summary—The E-R-I Model

So there you have it—the basic steps to applying the E-R-I model in your life, as described in the previous three chapters. Here's a summary of the three major steps.

1. Get rid of or control the emotions (E).

2. Apply your reason to do the following (R):

    • Recognize the reasons for a conflict.

- Have better communication.
- Consider and choose an effective conflict resolution style depending on the situation, your own style preferences, the other person's response, and other factors.

3. Use your intuition to help you do the following (I):
   - Better understand yourself and what's going on
   - Come up with possibilities and choose what to do.

In the next three sections, I'll explore more deeply how to use these techniques, and provide more specific examples of how to apply these techniques in different situations in your life.

**Section
Two**

Handling the Emotions

Recognizing the Reasons for a Conflict

Understanding the reasons for a conflict and the underlying needs fueling it will go a long way to help you resolve it.

Understanding Basic Needs and Wants

Conflicts often arise when people have underlying needs or strong wants that aren't being met, such as a desire for security, independence, or belonging. Conflicts also grow out of fears that something valuable may be lost, (e.g., a friendship, property, or peace and quiet). Such needs and fears easily fit into Abraham Maslow's well-known pyramid of needs (see next page), starting with survival, security, and safety on the bottom; then needs for friendship and belonging; above that needs for self-esteem, prestige, and achievement; and finally needs for self-actualization.

An unsatisfied need can be the source of a conflict. Recognizing that need and helping to satisfy it can be a means of resolving that conflict. On the surface, a conflict may appear unrelated to these needs. But unless these basic needs and wants are identified and dealt with, the conflict is apt to continue.

Need for self-actualization: Includes doing challenging projects, seeking opportunities for learning at a higher level. Associated with morality, creativity, problem solving, having a lack or prejudice, seeking for and accepting the facts.

Need for self-esteem: Includes working on important projects, seeking prestige and status, looking for recognition of one's strength and intelligence. Associated with confidence, achievement, respect of others, and respect by others.

Need for social belonging: Includes seeking acceptance, group membership, being associated with a successful team, looking for love and affection. Associated with friendship, family, and sexual intimacy.

Need for safety and security: Includes seeking physical safety, economic security, freedom from threats, comfort, and peace. Associated with seeking security of the body, of employment, of resources, of morality, of the family, of health and of property.

Need for physical survival: Includes the need for water, food, sleep, warmth, health, exercise, and sex. Associated with breathing, food, water, sleep, homeostasis, and excretion.

Sometimes underlying needs are expressed through strongly held, seemingly unchangeable positions, such as when two long-term employees are equally determined to get a higher position in the company. This can lead to an explosion of hostility that threatens the company's productivity, though the employees are motivated by different needs—one wants the higher position for the money due to growing financial burdens (a survival or security need), while the other is primarily motivated by the added responsibility and prestige of the higher position (the need for self-esteem and self-actualization). In this case, it might be possible to resolve the problem by recognizing these dynamics and perhaps finding a way to satisfy both, such as giving the employee seeking more responsibility the position, while finding a loan or extra work hours to satisfy the other.

These needs and wants can also affect how a person reacts (or over-reacts) to a situation, such as when you greet someone with a seemingly ordinary greeting, like: "Hiya Joe, what's new on the job?"—and unleash a wave of anger. Why the rage? Because Joe just had a fight with the boss and lost his job. You won't always know the reason for such an unexpected reaction in any encounter. But when that happens, you can learn not to take the response personally, so you don't get upset, or you can use the reaction to try to uncover what's really going on, such as by asking the person what you might have said to upset him. Then, the person might be open to sharing what's wrong or at least acknowledging that it was nothing you said. In short, one key in resolving a conflict is to recognize that true needs and fears often lie below the surface; if you can identify them—in yourself or the other person—that's a first step to a satisfying resolution.

Unfortunately, it may not always be obvious from the way a person acts or the position he or she takes in a conflict what those needs or fears are. People don't always want to reveal their true feelings. They might feel exposed or vulnerable, or worry that their true feelings will seem inappropriate or be misunderstood. Sometimes people aren't even aware of their true feelings—they just think they want or need something, and seek it without really understanding why. If they had a sense of their true motivation, they might look for—or be willing to accept—something else.

Hidden needs and agendas often keep the conflict pot stirred. For example:

- A husband fights with his wife because he doesn't want her to take a job, claiming the long hours would harm their young child, when his real reason is a fear that her success and skill would threaten his own competence. In response, she gets frustrated and resentful, instead of being able to address his fears while meeting her own needs.

- Neighbors battle over issues of noise and garbage, when the real issue is fear and misunderstanding about differences in lifestyles.

- In an office, an employee feuds with his co-workers and puts them down to his employer, claiming they are doing poor work, when he is worried about his own competence and feelings of low self-esteem. He tears down others in order to bolster up himself.

You probably can think of many other examples from your own experience of how unspoken needs and wants contribute to conflict. But people often don't recognize them, as Roger Fisher and William Ury explain in their book, *Getting to Yes* (New York: Penguin, 1983). They describe how many conflicts occur because people get stuck in positions and focus on upholding those positions, instead of recognizing the underlying needs or interests that have led them to adopt that position. Their wrong focus stands in their way of finding a solution, which depends on reconciling the underlying interests or needs of the parties involved.

As Fisher and Ury point out: "Reconciling interests rather than positions works for two reasons. First, for every interest there usually exist several possible positions that could satisfy it. All too often people simply adopt the most obvious position . . . But when you do look behind opposed positions or the motivating interests, you can often find an alternative position which meets not only your interests but theirs as well." That's because "behind opposed positions lie shared and compatible interests, as well as conflicting ones."

Thus, to resolve the conflict, look for the ways in which underlying needs are compatible or shared.

If you can sense what those needs or fears *are* in others or yourself, you can take them into consideration in working toward an effective resolution. If possible, bring them out in the open to discuss them. Or if a discussion isn't feasible, act in light of what you think those needs are to satisfy the other person. In turn, when you respond to the other's true needs, you can develop a stronger, closer, more mutually satisfying relationship.

Considering the other person's needs doesn't mean you should ignore your own, though there are times when the other person's needs are so much stronger than yours that you need to put your own needs aside for a time to help that person work through the conflict. Then, when the immediate conflict is over, you may find that your willingness to cater to the other person's needs has handsomely paid off in the other person's feelings of gratitude to you. Another pragmatic reason for putting the other person's needs first are that the other person is in a more powerful position than you, or that you have more to gain from the relationship than the other person. Ideally, look for creative solutions that satisfy both of your needs. But at times, address the other person's needs first, especially if he or she seems needy, or for other practical reasons.

At times when you don't have to put the other person's needs first, take some time to look at your *own* real needs and fears before trying to settle a conflict. This might lead you to find alternative ways to get these needs met or to overcome your fears. The two hostile employees struggling for a single position might have benefited from such an approach. Suppose that as one of those employees, you realize that your real reason for wanting that position is to gain more prestige, but in truth, you don't want the extra responsibility and time commitment. In this situation, you could then shift gears to go after what you really want, such as an enhancement in your current position, and you would now feel comfortable letting the other person get the promotion. The basis for the ongoing conflict with the other employee would be gone, and you might both end up with what you really want.

Thus, a key to achieving a resolution that works for everyone is to recognize the underlying needs or fears of yourself and others, so you can find responses that satisfy these needs or assuage these fears.

Recognizing Needs and Fears

A good example of how it's possible to resolve a crisis by tuning in to another person's needs and fears is illustrated by the story of Paula and Andrea. Andrea had a powerful need for belonging and a fear of being alone and being taken advantage of. As a result, when Paula acted as she usually did with other casual friends, unaware of Andrea's needs, this triggered a crisis in their relationship, which was only resolved after Paula became sensitive to Andrea's feelings and was able to discuss what happened.

Here's a brief summary of what happened. The problem started when Andrea returned to San Francisco after seven months out of town. She'd tried to set up a therapy-healing practice, but met numerous rebuffs, which left her feeling lonely and afraid. Also, she was upset by the impersonal, manipulative way that many people had treated her and the fact that many people tried to take advantage of her. They would attend some of her free introductory workshops but then not be available when she asked for their help in getting settled. Or they made promises, but didn't come through.

Thus, when she returned to San Francisco to do workshops and individual counseling again and called Paula, a casual acquaintance, about putting on some national programs and using a single coordinator to set up arrangements for them, Paula was delighted at the opportunity. Since Andrea had called over the Thanksgiving holidays, Paula suggested Andrea join her for a unique Thanksgiving dinner she was attending at a nearby church.

But what started as a friendly gesture turned into a disaster, though initially Paula couldn't understand why. First, as they got out of Paula's car about two blocks from the church, it was just starting to rain. As Paula walked quickly, holding the umbrella, Andrea walked along a step or two behind. Though Paula invited Andrea to come in under the umbrella a few times, Andrea didn't say anything and kept on walking a few paces behind. Then, at the church, where both paid for their dinners separately as they had agreed, Paula paid first and then walked ahead to look for seats for them, as she often did with other friends when they went to movies or other events together. Her other friends even appreciated her initiative in taking care of such arrangements.

Unfortunately, Andrea perceived Paula's actions quite differently. She was put off by the large impersonal setting of the dinner, since the long tables were set up in rows like in a charity soup kitchen instead of the warm, informal, friendly setting both had expected, and she also was upset when Paula didn't immediately see her. So she left the dinner before she even went in, telling the woman collecting money at the door: "I'm sorry, but I can't stay."

At first, Paula was perplexed by what happened, thinking Andrea simply left because the place looked like a soup kitchen. She had no idea that she contributed to the problem herself, until she called Andrea who sounded strangely cool and distant, and then explained "I felt so alienated and alone. You were always so far ahead of me. I felt abandoned."

Initially, Paula tried to explain rationally why she had gone ahead to reserve a table in the crowded dining room. But when Andrea continued to seem oddly distant, Paula realized there was something else going on, something deeper, and she asked Andrea, "Why did you feel abandoned?" Then, even though she thought there was no reason for Andrea to feel that way, Paula acknowledged and honored those feelings. Paula realized that Andrea needed to hear that she hadn't intended to abandon her, and that Paula really was concerned when she did not come back. So Paula began by telling Andrea about the many times she left the dinner to call her, reassuring her by saying, "I was really worried about you. I thought maybe you got sick. I looked for you until they told me you weren't coming back, and then I called you four times."

Then, as Andrea began to reveal how upset and sad she was, Paula listened, without trying to contradict her. She realized that what Andrea needed most was reassurance, support, and some evidence of Paula's care and concern. She also came to realize that Andrea's upset had started with the walk to the church in the rain, when Paula walked ahead so quickly, leaving Andrea feeling alienated, though Andrea did not know how to put her feelings of alienation into words. Then, her feelings of alienation and being left behind intensified when they paid separately—even though they agreed to do this in advance—and Paula bounded ahead into the room. So, as she explained to Paula, "I just needed to be back in the safety of the place I was staying. Everything seemed so alienating and degrading. I felt like I had been giving so much to help others with my work, and I suddenly felt so unappreci-ated. I felt like I was alone in a place that looked like a Salvation Army cafeteria, and I thought to myself: 'Am I reduced to this?' I felt so hope-less and worthless. I needed to escape; to be by myself."

Paula was able to salvage the situation by responding appropriately, validating and reassuring Andrea rather than firing back with her own resentment, even though she felt like she had done nothing wrong. Instead, she tried to see her own behavior from Andrea's point of view, saying how sorry she was that Andrea had gotten the wrong impression from what she did at the church, while encouraging Andrea to talk out her feelings to show she truly understood and appreciated her. So Paula managed to push the right buttons by being sensitive to what Andrea needed at the time, which was to feel listened to, understood, and important after having just returned to San Francisco.

The incident with Paula had triggered the response it did because at the time Andrea was already experiencing a great deal of loneliness, alienation, and sadness. She was especially sensitive, and ready to interpret what Paula did as another betrayal of trust and friendship. But Paula was able to overcome the conflict and break through the barrier of misunderstandings created by Andrea's special needs by being aware, ready to listen and respond, and by willing to see things from Andrea's point of view. So in the end, their friendship was restored, even deepened, and they were able to go on to plan future collaborations.

Should you be in a situation where someone becomes very emotional or appears to overact, this is generally an indicator that the situation has tapped into some deep inner needs. You may need to address these to resolve the problem and repair the relationship. In particular, you might keep in mind these considerations:

- If the person's reaction seems very intense and out of proportion to the kind of response expected in that situation, stop and think to yourself: What kind of deeper problems or needs might this reflect?

- Try to put yourself in the other person's shoes and imagine how things might look to this other person. What might this person be thinking about the situation?

- Consider your own behavior in light of the other person's point of view. Is there anything you might have done that could be misinterpreted?

- Consider whether the other person might be under special pressures right now that might have triggered the response.

- Think about what you might say to gently open up the possibility of talking about the real issues.

- Show that you are sensitive and really care about the other person and his or her point of view; indicate that you are willing to take the time to be patient and really understand.

- Be willing to put your own needs aside to put a priority on listening to the other person's concerns. Later on you can express your own needs; right now, show the other person you value him or her and want to satisfy his or her needs, especially when he or she seems to be in very much pain.

Meeting Mutual Needs

In the previous case, the conflict was resolved because one person put her own needs on hold to focus on the more serious needs of the other. But many times in a conflict, your own needs are equally important, although you still have to meet the other person's needs to solve the problem. In this case, a key to resolution is finding an approach that can satisfy both of you by examining the real needs underlying the apparent cause of the conflict.

A situation like this took place between Julie and her landlord,

Tanya. Tanya lived upstairs in the townhouse the two women shared. Julie had been living there for about two years, and had every intention of staying, since she was in a graduate program at a nearby school, and felt the apartment was ideal for her needs. She also felt she had developed a good, friendly relationship with her landlord. About a year earlier, the original one-year lease had expired, and Julie had stayed on a month-by-month basis in what seemed like a satisfactory arrangement for everyone.

The problem started when Tanya said she wanted to draw up a lease, just to protect herself in case Julie moved out suddenly without sufficient notice. However, while Julie expected Tanya to simply reformalize their existing arrangement and was perfectly satisfied to sign a one- or two-year lease, Tanya brought an agreement with a number of changes. Not only did Tanya up the rent 14 percent on the grounds that the place was a bargain (it would have rented for much more on the open market), but she wanted an extra $1,500 security deposit. Also, she wanted a written request from Julie to hold the workshops Julie occasionally hosted at the house. Tanya assured her: "I'll normally say yes. I just want to know what's going on." But Julie was incensed that Tanya now demanded a written notice about an activity she had been carrying on for two years without any problem. Finally, she was angered by a penalty clause stating that if the rent wasn't paid by the fifth day of the month, there would be a $100 penalty, plus 8 percent monthly interest, and if a check bounced, Tanya wanted $20 for check costs.

When Julie expressed some of her concerns, particularly about the extra money, Tanya just brushed them off, citing the letter of the law. For example, Tanya told Julie that she and her husband could set any rent they wanted in an owner-occupied building and that Julie would get her security deposit back on moving, assuming no damage. Then Tanya left the contract for her to review.

When Julie reviewed the contract, she was even more upset. The more she thought about it, the more she found the contract and her exchange with Tanya disturbing. Both were overly impersonal, mean-spirited, and implied suspicion about everything she did, though she had been living as Tanya's tenant for over two years without any problems. But now Tanya seemed to treat her as if she were just anyone walking in off the street.

So the next day, Julie wrote Tanya a letter expressing her feelings.

Though she allowed that she could probably manage the higher-than-usual rent increase, she described why she didn't feel comfortable with the other lease provisions. She concluded by stating that although she had been planning to stay for at least another two years, she had decided to move and was giving her thirty-day notice.

Julie's decision to move was exactly what Tanya *didn't* want. What she did want was a firmer commitment from Julie to stay there and wanted to be sure that if Julie did move she wouldn't do so suddenly or without cleaning up the place, making it difficult to show the place and find a new tenant quickly. But instead, the lease and the exchange about it made Julie feel as if Tanya viewed her like a stranger coming to rent an apartment and her only concern was the dollar sign. She felt humiliated and demeaned, not even considering the extra financial burden.

Unfortunately, when Tanya saw Julie's letter, not recognizing Julie's needs, all she could see was that Julie's moving confirmed why she needed the lease. When she called Julie about the letter, she accused her of taking advantage by moving right before Christmas, the worst possible time to rent the place. Tanya didn't realize that Julie was moving because of the way she changed the terms of the lease and treated her. So each of them was upset and blamed the other for the outcome neither wanted—Julie moving. They practically hung up on each other. Each still thought it was a dispute about money and legal terms in a lease, when it was about much more: both parties' unexpressed needs.

The situation might have ended on this sad note, with Julie moving at this worst possible time for them both. However, because she was so busy right then, Julie wrote a note asking for a few extra days or even weeks to get her things organized, pointing out that it would give Tanya more time to show the place. And as a final thought, she opened up the door to a discussion by adding: "Perhaps we might also talk about reactions to the lease you left me, so you don't feel I'm trying to take advantage of you. I actually felt you were trying to do this to me. Apart from any financial considerations, the provisions in the new lease made me uncomfortable about staying here for various reasons."

The letter was just what was needed, since it opened the door for Julie and Tanya to discuss their real needs, so both could get what they really wanted. After she saw the letter, Tanya called Julie to set up a meeting, and Julie agreed. They met in Julie's apartment. Tanya explained her concerns and fears that led her to write up such a strict lease, noting how everything was going wrong in her life at the time. A close relative had died, she had unexpected difficulties at work, and there were other family problems, leading her to want more stability and security in her life. Apologetically, she concluded: "I wasn't really thinking about how you might feel about it, and I really feel you are a good tenant and want you to stay. The lease wasn't meant as an ultimatum, just something for you to look at so we could talk about it. Maybe we can still work things out, if you'd consider staying."

The result of Tanya's revelations about her own problems and her appreciation for Julie worked like magic. Within ten minutes, the two women had easily worked out an agreement, since their real desires and needs were actually complementary. Julie agreed to make sure the apartment was in reasonable shape for showing, and Tanya dropped the rent increase, the permission clause and the penalty clause, assuring Julie these had been triggered by unrelated, personal fears. So Julie finally agreed to stay and sign the lease, and just as important as the financial concessions were the assurances Tanya gave Julie that she was a valued person and tenant. Thus, by opening themselves up and sharing what they really needed and wanted, both Julie and Tanya were able to satisfy their mutual needs, and as a result of the near disaster, both came to appreciate each other more.

This process of discovering needs underlying a conflict may sometimes seem like uncovering clues in a mystery. But there are steps you can take to make the process less of a guessing game and more of a sure way to recognizing the true problem, so you can resolve it.

Often, a conflict may appear to be a win-lose situation—i.e., the tenant pays more or less rent, and the landlord gets more or less money. But as the story of Julia and Tanya illustrates, the true problems or issues may lie beneath the surface. Each person may have certain important needs he or she wants to satisfy (such as long-term stability or feeling needed and valued). If these needs can be uncovered, it suddenly becomes possible to satisfy both parties. Thus, a key to resolving conflict is finding an opening to bring up those needs (such as writing a letter to invite discussion) and getting away from the original positions where both persons are stuck to find alternative solutions.

To this end, keep in mind the following guidelines for getting unstuck by responding to mutual needs.

- If you feel someone's initial position is impossible for you, but there might be something to gain if you can soften that position, don't take that position as an ultimatum.

- Open up the door to further discussion if possible, say by writing a letter or making a phone call to talk about the situation and seek some mutually satisfying resolution.

- Find out why the person has taken the position he or she has; look for the person's real needs underneath.

- Think about your own underlying needs; ask what is really most important to you.

- Consider some possibilities that might satisfy both of your needs. Or think about ways to give up some things that are less important to you and more important to the other person in return for getting things that are more important to you and less so for the other.

- Share your concerns calmly and listen respectfully. Emphasize your desire to solve the problem and focus on solutions, not recriminations and anger over what has happened before.

Discovering Hidden Needs and Fears

In the previous examples, it was possible to resolve a conflict by getting needs and fears out in the open so they could be discussed and resolved. Once everybody's true concerns were addressed, the conflict melted away, and the people in these examples developed warmer relationships due to the conflict. The resolution process triggered a revelation of needs that led to greater openness and shared understandings.

However, such a revelation is often hard to achieve. People in conflict often conceal their real needs and fears or fail to recognize them. The conflicts in their lives continue until these real needs are discovered and addressed. It may become necessary to dig deep to discover what's going on in the other person, in yourself, or both. Sometimes it may be better to let the other person hold onto a fiction if he or she doesn't want to admit his real needs or fears—like the person who feels better imagining himself a strong solid rock for his family and would be literally crushed to realize that others don't rely on him as much as he believes. But if you sense that these underlying needs or fears are really motivating the person, you need to take into consideration these underlying sources of motivation rather than the apparent needs or fears that are being expressed.

This process of discovery is what helped Arlene achieve a satisfactory ghostwriting arrangement with a family counselor, Mary Beth. Mary Beth had repeatedly changed her mind about what type of writing arrangement she wanted: a co-authorship where she paid less and gave up half of the royalties; a ghostwriting-but-shared-royalty arrangement where she paid more in return for the writer taking a smaller percentage of the royalties; or a straight ghostwriting-for-a-higher-fee arrangement, which strained her budget.

The arrangement started successfully after Mary Beth hired Arlene to ghostwrite a proposal for a book on relationships, with Mary Beth supplying the notes and transcripts for counseling sessions. But the conflict started after Arlene helped find a publisher. Unfortunately, the $3000 advance wouldn't fully cover Arlene's ghostwriter fee, and finding a publisher with a higher advance was iffy. At first, it seemed that Arlene had proposed a good solution; she would work for half of her usual fee in return for half of the royalties and her name on the book as the writer "with" Mary Beth. Arlene viewed her proposal as a business proposition and thought it especially fair, since she gave Mary Beth the option to change her mind at any time before the book contract was signed and simply pay Arlene her regular ghostwriter fee.

But Mary Beth was furious about the proposal. She complained that Arlene was asking for too much money and credit, while Mary Beth not only was spending time providing the information, but had expenses for transcripts and typing. Though Arlene tried offering different formulas for apportioning costs and credits, none worked, because the two women understood the issue differently. To Arlene, it was simply the negotiation of a business deal. Her main interest was getting paid, while the credit was at least something to show for the risk she took if there was no money beyond the advance. To Mary Beth, the book was an extension of her identity and she had a huge emotional investment in it.

So the conflict escalated, because the two were coming from such very different places. Since Arlene initially was unaware of Mary Beth's concerns, she found it very difficult to talk to her. Each time she offered another suggestion about how the two might work together, she felt like she was walking on eggs, since almost anything could set Mary Beth off. In turn, Mary Beth began questioning Arlene's integrity, wondering if Arlene would bill her for the correct number of hours on the project and how she would know. At the same time, with her tight budget, Mary Beth wavered about what to do: to pay more up front for

Arlene taking less royalty and credit, or pay less and give up more roy-alty and control.

Finally, after two months of wrangling, just as it came time to reach an agreement or abandon the book, Arlene suggested an alternative that seemed acceptable: If Arlene could be listed as a co-author and share the royalties equally, Mary Beth wouldn't have to pay her any-thing more, beyond covering any additional out-of-pocket expenses. Though it was Arlene's least desired alternative, since in return for the extra credit, she would get no more money if the book didn't do well, at least Mary Beth agreed so the book could go forward. But when it came to signing the contract, Mary Beth balked, coming up with all sorts of reasons why she felt uncomfortable working with Arlene and didn't trust her, when in fact the underlying reason was that she didn't want to share co-authorship and control.

Just as it looked like things were going to fall apart for good, Arlene sensed what was really going on with Mary Beth. Outwardly, Mary Beth indicated that she was concerned about the money, and acted to keep down the amount of money she spent by agreeing to the co-authorship arrangement. But in reality, she wanted the credit and to maintain her control and ownership of the book. She was literally at war with herself. While her inner self was fighting against giving up this power, her outer self was seeking to do this to save money. The insight came to Arlene in a flash and it led her to act to save her rela-tionship with Mary Beth and the book. She spoke to Mary Beth's real needs and fears, explaining:

"Look, I really don't need the credit. I'm not trying to take this book away from you. I just asked for the percentage and credits because of the extra risk I'm taking in not getting paid. But I don't want the credit. This is your book."

And with that, the tension that had been building vanished. Arlene's statement was right on target, and suddenly Mary Beth real-ized what she really wanted—the credit, ownership, and control of this book. The money issue was less important. She wanted this to fully be her own book.

The result was that Arlene and Mary Beth finally did work out an agreement. Arlene became a ghostwriter again, as they had arranged in the beginning. But to deal with Mary Beth's concerns about money, Arlene would receive only half of the payment on completing the manuscript, the rest on acceptance.

In the end, the book did go forward. The conflict was resolved by Arlene recognizing that Mary Beth's inner needs and fears were at war with her external concerns: her inner conflict needed to be resolved first in order to resolve the external conflict. Mary Beth's concerns over money had masked what really mattered—the credit and control of the book. The book had to be hers alone, and ghostwriting was the only way to go.

Similarly, if you are in a situation where someone is very emotional about something, seems ambivalent about what he or she wants, and you are having a difficult time in achieving a mutually beneficial resolution, take the time to look underneath the surface for hidden needs or fears. Some ways to do this include the following:

- Look for clues that suggest what the person may really want, but hasn't admitted to you or to him- or herself. Notice what the person is resisting or gets upset about as a clue to what he really doesn't want, even though he claims that is what he wants (e.g., Mary Beth saying she wanted the co-authorship agreement to save money, when she really needed the credit and control).

- Come up with a suggested proposal you think might meet those hidden needs. If the person feels it does, the proposal might break a logjam. If not, the person can always turn the proposal down. (This is what Arlene did by saying that she really didn't want the credit and had just asked for it because of her extra financial risk, while emphasizing that it was Mary Beth's book.)

- Put your own needs on the table, because you want your own needs satisfied too, as well as satisfying the other person. Once everybody's true needs are out in the open, you are both in a better position to come up with alternatives that will be satisfying to you both. (For example, this is what Arlene did when she emphasized that her first interest was making money and the credit was secondary. Once both sets of needs were on the table, they were obviously compatible, since credit and control came first for Mary Beth, while the money came first for Arlene. So now they could work together and get what they each really wanted—not a co-authorship that neither wanted.)

Putting the Other's Needs First

While it can be a difficult breakthrough to recognize another person's true needs and act on them, the toughest challenge can be those situations where you have to recognize the *priority* of someone else's needs over your own. Sometimes, this recognition can be the only effective way to resolve the conflict when the other person is needier at the moment, more emotionally upset about the situation, or has more power than you. These are compelling reasons to satisfy the other person's needs or fears first, so you can move on to working out a rational resolution to the problem. This does *not* mean giving up on your own needs. It just means you may need to put them off for a while, get them met in a more indirect or roundabout way from this person, or find a way to get these needs met somewhere else.

That's what happened for Sally, who felt tangled in a bureaucratic snarl when an official who didn't like her made things difficult for her. The problem began when Sally was ready to begin an extern position in her psychology program. She described what she wanted to the placement director, Mr. Washington, who suggested a work program in which Sally would work part-time in a halfway house for substance abusers.

Though the program sounded like an ideal way to get some hands-on experience in a field that fascinated her, Sally soon found the job was not what she expected. Instead of spending her time helping in therapy sessions or talking one-on-one with patients, she was assigned to do many center chores, like preparing meals and doing gardening in the yard.

When Sally spoke to Mr. Washington about being placed in another program, he at first tried to convince her to work things out where she was by talking to the director at the center, explaining that it was hard to find new placements in the middle of the term. But Sally insisted that she had already tried to make changes and felt insulted and demeaned in her role, until finally after a heated discussion, Mr. Washington agreed to find her something else. After a few weeks of his calling around unsuccessfully, she began to make a few calls and found what seemed like the perfect solution—another drug program with outpatients, but one where she could assist with intake interviews, facilitating group sessions, and help in the recreational program.

However, when she met with Mr. Washington to tell him the good news and arrange for the placement, he announced with enthusiasm that he had found another program for her after extensive efforts. In fact, to speed up the change, he had enrolled her in the program and completed all the paperwork. Now all she had to do was sign the necessary agreements, and she could begin.

Unfortunately, instead of trying to talk calmly about the two options, Sally became very upset. She spoke with growing intensity of her need to find a proper placement and the benefits of the responsibility and training offered by the place she had found, and she aired her uncertainties about the place Mr. Washington had found. She also complained that the school had been at fault in not initially finding her the proper placement, and slow in finding her a new one. Meanwhile, as the discussion heated up, Mr. Washington accused Sally of being very inflexible and said maybe he should terminate her from the entire program. Sally finally stormed out of his office in a rage.

It was at this point that she came to me for advice on what to do. While the offer to get into the program Mr. Washington had found was still available, she really wanted to get into the program she had found. She felt that Mr. Washington was blocking the way, insisting that she go into the program he had found for her and unwilling to consider her suggestion, because he didn't like her. She felt he resented her independence and determination because he felt students should be docile, and she wondered if she should now go over his head and appeal to the school's field committee. As Sally went on, she made it clear she was gearing up for an all-out battle with Mr. Washington, and the school if necessary, to assert her rights. In her view, the placement director insulted her, was prejudiced against her, and was about to terminate her from the school's placement program because she dared to be independent.

Though many of her points were valid, was this confrontation the best strategy to get what she wanted? Couldn't that lead to Mr. Washington being even more defensive and set in his position? Besides, he *had* tried to find her another placement that was more suitable. Shouldn't he be recognized and validated for that? Then, too, regardless of Sally's personal feelings, Mr. Washington had the advantage of power in the situation, since he was in the position to approve or deny her access to the school placement program. It was in her best interest to be on his good side and avoid a direct confrontation, because if the situation escalated into an official challenge to his power, most probably Mr. Washington would win.

Thus, it seemed that the best strategy for getting what she wanted—the placement she had found—was to look at the issue from Mr. Washington's point of view. What might address *his* needs? Though Sally had her own needs (to be independent and self-fulfilled in her work), these needs were probably best met by taking care of Mr. Washington's needs first. He would then be in a position to help *her*.

One of his key needs, it seemed, was to feel in control, but it seemed that in her confrontations with him, she had angered him by challenging his authority in her determined efforts to take the initiative. So what she probably needed to do was the opposite of what she proposed. Instead of coming on strong and threatening to exercise her legal rights, which could possibly escalate the confrontation, she should probably approach him contritely and apologetically. She should appear conciliatory and indicate she was very sorry if she seemed to challenge him. Also, she might acknowledge his efforts on her behalf to secure her a better placement. Then, after she had cooled things down and led Mr. Washington to understand that she recognized and appreciated his efforts, she might gently explain how she had gotten so upset because she found a program she really liked and felt was very appropriate for her. Besides, she might point out that this program would contribute to her learning at the school, which was one of his objectives for his students.

Thus, since the key issue from Mr. Washington's point of view seemed to be a student challenging an administrator's authority, her strategy should be to acknowledge and accept his authority and show her contrition in trying to challenge him, even though she might feel it humbling or even humiliating to do so. "Throw yourself at this man's mercy; acknowledge his power; reinforce his authority; show your appreciation; seek his forgiveness. You might feel angry and hurt yourself, but think of how this will help you satisfy your own need, since you are apt to get more by seeing the struggle from his point of view. And as the person in power, he has the most power to decide the outcome of the situation," I advised her.

Sally decided to use the strategy I suggested. She wrote Mr. Washington a gentle, apologetic letter to smooth the way, and when she met with him, she used the conciliatory approach we had discussed. And it worked like magic. At once, Mr. Washington softened. He said that perhaps he had been too harsh in threatening to terminate her from the program. He admitted that he should have been more appreciative of her initiative in trying to find a better program. Accordingly, he agreed to meet with the director of the program she had located and if the arrangements met with the school standards, he would be pleased to have her enter the program. In fact, he stated that if the program was up to standards, he might be able to include it in the range of programs offered to other students who sought placements—and if so, he would have Sally to thank for that.

About a week later, Mr. Washington approved her placement. By giving Mr. Washington what he wanted or needed in their confrontation—acknowledgement and acceptance of his control and authority—Sally ended up getting her own way. The resolution hinged on meeting *his* needs, since he was the one in power, and on *her* ability to read his needs and address them in such a way as to meet her own ends. Sally's situation might have ended up badly had the conflict continued to escalate. Then, she surely wouldn't have gotten what she wanted. Instead, there was a win-win resolution for them both.

If you are in a situation where it seems necessary to first satisfy the other person's needs to resolve the conflict, and the other person is in a position of power (leaving you unable to force through your own agenda or walk away from the problem), some keys to achieving a satisfying resolution include the following:

- Notice what the other person's needs are from what the person is saying or doing (i.e., being in control of the situation; achieving your acquiescence to his power).

- If you aren't clear what the other person's needs are, ask questions to find out what he or she wants and listen carefully to what he or she says. Sometimes the person may be clear in stating personal needs; other times these needs may be buried between the lines, and you may need to use your intuition to find them. (Some questions to a person in a power position might be: "What would you like me to do?" "How can I help you achieve———?" "Is there something I did that is bothering you?")

- If you feel that a key issue for this person is being in control or a fear of being challenged—and that person is in a position of power relative to you—be humble, apologetic, and self-effacing if necessary—help that person feel more secure, powerful, and unchallenged. Being tough in such a situation is only apt to make that person become defensive and respond by showing how he or she can exert power over you, which will very likely mean not giving you what you want. Once the other person feels secure in his or her power, you can calmly, rationally, and gently ask for what you really want in a way that shows deference. In simpler terms, by massaging the other person's feelings, he or she will be more likely to accede to your request. After all, giving you what you want from a position of power is a way of affirming that power. In short, by giving up your own power, you can help yourself get what you want in such a situation. Showing off your power may prevent you from achieving your goal. You'll probably just escalate the conflict and not get what you want.

Summing Up

Looking for the underlying needs of both you and the other party can be a key to resolving some conflicts. As the foregoing examples illustrate, there are four key considerations when you do this:

1. Recognizing another person's needs and fears, then talking about them and responding to them, can sometimes be enough to resolve the conflict.

2. Recognizing the other's needs and sharing your own needs can sometimes allow you to work out an arrangement that satisfies you both.

3. At times, you may have to look for hidden needs and fears that underlie stated ones in order to respond to the real needs and fears that are producing the conflict.

4. Sometimes, you may have to place a priority on resolving the other party's needs first in order to satisfy your own.

Dealing with Your Own Angers and Fears

Feelings of anger and fear can easily build up in any conflict situation and further fuel the conflict. Earlier, I discussed the importance of both letting go of your own anger and letting others release angry, negative feelings to clear the way towards a resolution. But sometimes it can be hard to release those negative emotions, so this chapter will teach you various techniques for dealing with your own anger and fear.

While you want to take the other person's needs and desires into consideration in the hopes of furthering a relationship, it is equally important to take care of yourself. While it might be ideal for the other person to listen and consider your needs, too, others may be unaware of them or set on their own positions and goals, causing your own angers and fears to build up. But you can learn to control—and overcome—these blocks to a successful resolution.

Releasing Anger

A critical step to solving any conflict and renewing a good relationship is letting go of anger—both yours and the other person's. Sometimes this means putting your anger aside, as when you make yourself listen to the other person's tirade for a bit. But ultimately you have to acknowledge your own anger and deal with it more effectively. The key is to learn to release it with control.

The wrong way to release your anger is to attack or explode with it, as often happens in long-term personal relationships or at work. In both of those situations feelings of anger can build up over the months and years. A typical instance might be the couple who have been together for years. When they have a fight, the anger escalates as one or both start bringing up everything the other person has ever done wrong in the past. This kind of attack does nothing to solve the immediate conflict or defuse the anger. Each person just gets more upset and angry; the only way to resolve the problem is by calming down. Yet when you ignore or deny your anger, you can end up feeling as frustrated as when you are yelling at others and they are yelling back, without resolving the conflict that triggered this outburst.

But with some internal processing, you can reduce or eliminate your anger and take care of your frustration at the same time. You can work on this even as you listen to the other person vent his or her built-up emotions. Ideally, you will then both be ready to move past the anger (which you defused, and he or she vented) and deal with the conflict.

Letting Go of Your Anger

One way to deal with your anger is to release it internally through a *visualization* or a *releasing ritual*. This is especially effective when it isn't appropriate to vent anger to others, such as your boss, or when you realize that expressing anger will only escalate an already volatile situation.

In a visualization, you see yourself doing or experiencing something in your mind's eye, such as imagining that you are expressing the anger you feel towards a person. You achieve a feeling of release, but don't get in trouble by expressing your anger openly. A releasing ritual involves a similar process, except that you act out your feelings in a private place. At times you need this kind of personal release so your anger can safely pass through you and be released.

There are a number of ways to do visualizations or releasing rituals. Some of these were mentioned in Chapter 2, but they are reviewed here as a reminder. Choose those which feel most comfortable to you or create your own.

Getting Rid of the Anger by Grounding It Out

Visualize anger coming into you like a beam of negative energy from the person or situation that triggered it. Then imagine this energy moving downward within you and dispersing harmlessly into the ground.

Getting Rid of the Anger by Projecting It Out and Eliminating It

Get into a very relaxed state and imagine that you are sending out your anger and projecting it onto a screen. Next, imagine taking a ray-gun or bow and arrow, and shooting at that anger—an especially good approach for destroying your more violent urges! Each time you zap the anger with your gun or bow and arrow, you experience the anger releasing and draining away.

Cleansing Your Energy to Shake Off Your Anger

Another way to get rid of anger or other negativity is to cleanse the energy field or aura around you. To do this, stand or sit up straight and rub your hands over your head. Imagine that these gestures are clearing out the energy field around this part of your body. As you move your hands, feel yourself drawing the angry or other negative feelings out of yourself, and then shake them away with your hands.

Releasing the Anger by Cutting the Other Person Down to Size

As discussed in Chapter 2, you can also release your anger against a particular person by making that person seem smaller, and therefore less important to you. This technique can be especially appropriate when you keep dwelling on that person and he or she looms large in your life, whether you are involved a particular conflict now or not.

Begin by seeing yourself talking to this person. See him or her doing whatever makes you angry—such as lying, not listening to you, acting like a know-it-all, or whatever. As you talk, watch this person shrinking in size. Notice his or her voice becoming fainter and fainter. Soon he or she should begin to seem *much* less important or powerful to you.

Then, when you see yourself leaving this tiny person, you should feel very powerful. Or if you prefer, imagine this person becoming so small that he becomes like a puddle, one you can step in or splash under your feet. So again, you have put this person in his place.

As with any of these techniques, repeat the process if memories of the situation or person come back. It may take some repetition if your anger has been building up for some time. But gradually, as you work with this release process, the anger and bitterness you feel will melt away. The person or situation might even seem funny to you.

Getting Rid of Your Anger by Learning from the Situation

Still another anger release method is to look at the situation which has caused you to feel anger or other negative emotions and ask yourself: "What can I learn about dealing with future situations from this? How can I make sure I don't have this kind of problem again?"

This approach can help you release your anger because it gives you some productive ways to deal with what has happened. It also helps you learn how better to deal with a negative situation in the future and view whatever happened as something productive and even positive. Don't view the conflict or situation as a waste of time and effort. Instead, see it as a chance to learn and grow. When you come to this realization, you will feel a release of anger. Through learning, you have transformed your anger into something positive and productive.

Protecting Yourself from Negative People

Some people are just plain negative. If you find yourself around someone who is consistently angry, hostile, argumentative, critical, or otherwise troublesome to deal with, you need to set up some psychological barriers or protections against this person. These barriers can be particularly useful if you have to be around a negative person on a daily basis and you can't simply end the connection, as with a co-worker or nearby relative. But by putting up a guard surrounding yourself, you can shut out the feelings of negativity you experience around this person.

It is important to do this because being around such a person can pull you down and may easily suck you into a conflict. To prevent this, you can create a mental wall of energy around yourself to keep out the negativity. Whenever you feel threatened by this potential negativity, you put up the wall. You can be selective in when you do this, so your wall doesn't push away everyone—just the person or persons you feel are negative and threaten your positive feelings.

A way to create this wall is to imagine a white light of pure, positive energy around yourself. Or see yourself in a protective bubble. Or visualize yourself as a duck, and see the negativity, like water, running off your back. You can use many possible visualizations, as long as you use an image to create a zone of protection around yourself. Then, whenever you feel threatened by any negative energy from someone, put up your shield to ward it off or even send it back to the person from whom it comes. You'll feel more centered and grounded, and can more calmly and comfortably do whatever you need to do.

Learning to Let Go of Difficult Relationships

Another way to deal with problem relationships is to let the relationship go when you can. If you find that a person is too negative or the relationship has been rocky for some time, think about whether you really need that relationship. If not, end it—and perhaps do a visualization of release to see it gone. Or at least minimize your contact and find alternative things to do to replace being with that person.

It may also be appropriate to let go of the relationship if you find that the other person is holding you back. He or she might have a certain conception of who you are, although you see yourself differently or have changed. This identity problem is one that often comes up when you go through a period of change or self-development and the people you have been around aren't ready to accept your change. Should this happen, you might need to let them go or at least pull away from them for a time. Create a protective distance between you and the relationship. If you do need to make any contact, try a visualization to help you keep your emotional distance when you meet.

For example, at one workshop I led, a woman who had gone through a personal development program found she had to create more distance between herself and her mother. They continually argued and her mother had a very negative, grim way of looking at the world. As the woman explained, her mother's point of view soon undermined her positive feelings after just a short time of being in her presence. The more sensitive and aware she became as she changed, the more deeply wounded she felt by her mother's negativity and the more she needed to disconnect. As the woman described her situation:

Ever since I have been young, I have had this war with my mother, because she has this very negative way of looking at everything. So she thinks that everything that can go wrong in your life will go wrong.

It became even more difficult to have a relationship with her as I started to become more sensitive. I increasingly found it difficult to be around her for more than about an hour or two, or I would start to feel irritable, depressed, and hostile. So I found I had to set up all these protections and barriers around myself to keep her negativity from affecting me, but after a few hours, it felt draining to keep up this wall, so I began to see her less and less. I found reasons why I couldn't come and visit or ways to cut the visit short. And this approach helped me to feel much better. Though I couldn't make a complete break, I felt much freer than ever before. It was like I had left her prison.

Likewise, if you can't resolve the conflict in a relationship, you may have to break away or reduce the time you spend with the person.

Similarly, if you find that people at work are standing in the way of your success by having an attitude that puts you down, such as by repeatedly telling you that you can't do something or urging you not to think so big, then let them go.

In short, if you find yourself around a negative person who is putting or pulling you down, consider letting that relationship go, particularly if the negativity is very strong or your efforts to put up mental protections don't work. Instead, it may be time to walk away—or if a total break isn't feasible, cut down the time you spend together. To whatever extent possible, cut this person out of your life and let go.

Learning Not to Take It Personally

Another strategy that can help you avert conflicts is to distance yourself from the situation. Learn not to take a conflict personally. This way, you can sidestep some problems and feel good about yourself at the same time. This approach also serves to remind you of this helpful truth— that another person's negative behavior is often not directed specifically at you. He or she might be acting this way due to a personal problem that has nothing to do with you. So why take it on?

This don't-take-it-personally approach can be particularly useful in casual encounters. You may come up against a person who is feeling angry about some situation, and your appearance triggers an angry response. While it may be easy to respond with your own justifiable anger, that's a sure way to begin—and keep building—a serious conflict. If you can learn to respond by not taking such anger personally, you may be able to pass the conflict by, as well as raise your self-esteem—and even preserve your relationship with the other person, if you want to preserve it.

For example, one woman in a workshop described how she got upset after a bus driver snapped at her when she tried to give a man who seemed confused some information on where to go. As she explained: "I told the bus driver I was just trying to help, but the driver was furious, telling me that the man had been on the bus before and he knew exactly where to drop the man off. So I was wrong and should just keep quiet."

The woman felt like yelling back at the driver, although she said nothing, and she was upset for the next few hours, because the driver's attitude had made her feel stupid and humiliated.

In such a situation, it's appropriate to back off. The woman probably wouldn't want to confront the driver over his nasty attitude towards her. That might only create a more heated confrontation, and she had nothing to gain from standing up to the driver, except perhaps salving her wounded pride. But she could do that for herself by not taking the encounter personally.

To help herself depersonalize the incident, she might consider that perhaps the bus driver reacted as he did because he was already feeling tense and under pressure for any number of reasons, such as people repeatedly asking him the same questions and telling him again and again where to stop. Plus he might be tense due to traffic jams, drivers cutting him off, and so forth. He may feel irritable and may also feel a loss of power because of all these pressures. As a result, should a rider start giving information about where to get off to someone else, he might perceive it as a threat to his own role, infuriating him. And maybe other pressures at home or work happened to darken his day.

Then, having considered these possibilities, the woman could feel less tense by realizing she has done nothing wrong; his response was his problem, and not talking back to him was the right thing to do. By going through this process, the woman will feel empowered, not demeaned, by the encounter. She just had to take the time to run over the experience in her head to convince herself of this.

The woman on the bus was in a situation where she could easily walk away. But even if you can't do so because of an ongoing relationship, depersonalization works. The key is learning to separate yourself from the problem so you feel it's outside of you; then you can approach it in a neutral way and avoid self-blame. Plus you might find positive ways to view the experience as a lesson for the future or as a way to strengthen your techniques of visualization and conflict management.

Even if in thinking honestly about a situation, you decide you were *not* right, being detached helps. It makes it easier to acknowledge that you screwed up, and helps you decide what to do about it. The process makes you more flexible and objective, so you can not only better resolve this particular problem, but can also apply this approach in dealing with other conflicts in the future.

Gain Some Mental Justice

Sometimes nothing soothes anger as well as thoughts of gaining justice. You might consider this a form of justified revenge, a kind of mental retribution. This can help you feel better about the situation, without resorting to real violence to release your feelings of anger. Real revenge or retribution might be a poor strategy anyway, since it will just escalate the conflict. On the other hand, if you imagine taking some action to punish or get back at whoever wronged you, you may feel better without endangering yourself or others.

While some people may find this method works as a useful release, some may find that thinking violent or angry thoughts increases their frustration. So only use these techniques if they seem to relieve your tension; don't use them if they serve to refocus your anger and increase your irritation level.

Some people believe this mental processing can have a real physical effect by either affecting how you relate to the person who wronged you or by affecting the wrongdoer directly in some way. But leaving metaphysical results aside, the process of seeking mental justice may at least serve as a release if this technique works for you. The way it works is that you direct your hostile feelings about the situation mentally at the wrongdoer instead of inward, toward yourself. Then, as you direct your feelings outward, you feel a tremendous emotional release and liberation.

One woman did this when her neighbor clipped off the top of a tree on her property, which obscured his scenic view, when she was away on a vacation. Though he denied having trimmed the tree in her absence, she was still convinced he had done it. She stewed about it for months, feeling further confrontations with him hopeless. Also, she was afraid of doing anything in retaliation, since he might respond in kind, say by trimming even more of her trees.

She was finally able to release this accumulated negative energy in a workshop by going into a relaxed state where she found a power animal, a gorilla, who would help her deal with this neighbor. In her mind, she saw the gorilla lumber over to the neighbor's property, where he climbed up the neighbor's prize tree and tore off the foliage, then ripped up the neighbor's lawn and garden before running off. Lastly, the gorilla climbed her own battered tree and patted it with his hands, as if to heal it.

As a result of this visualization, the woman suddenly felt much better. She had let go of the built-up anger inside her, so her healing process could begin, symbolized by the image of the gorilla patting her tree with healing energy. In fact, the woman felt so much better that she approached her neighbor the next day after returning home from work. She told the neighbor firmly that she knew he had clipped her tree no matter what he claimed, and that he should stay off her property in the future—or else. Then, feeling restored and free of the anger of the past, she returned home able to put the problem out of her mind for a while. Although the problem with her neighbor flared up again when he stopped by to complain about her tree several weeks later, the visualization gave her some temporary respite.

To achieve mental justice, simply go through a visualization in which you imagine yourself, or someone acting for you, taking some action to appropriately punish the person who has wronged you. It's even fun to think of what you might do to achieve the appropriate justice. Begin the process by getting very relaxed in a quiet place. A dark room can help you tap into your intuitive, unconscious mind. Then, take a few deep breaths as you concentrate on your breathing.

When you feel very relaxed, mentally ask yourself the question: 'What can I do to get a just punishment for _____?' Fill in the blank with a capsule description of the situation. Then, observe what happens. You will probably see yourself enjoying the other person receiving an appropriate punishment. Later, when you come back to normal consciousness, notice if you feel better about the situation. If you do feel less tension and are in a better mood, this is a good technique for you to continue to use. But if the anger is still there, use a different anger-releasing or transforming approach.

Another way to gain mental justice is to take some conscious, symbolic action to experience it, again noting if this is an effective releaser for you. If so, continue to use this technique and if not, don't. Some possible symbolic actions might be to write a nasty letter (but don't send it), or to plot out a scenario of the things you would like to do if you could (such as embarrassing the person who insulted you publicly by having him parade naked down the street).

Still another effective method for some people is to create a symbolic mental justice ritual. You choose certain ritual words or paraphernalia, create a ritual setting to intensify your feelings and promote an altered state of consciousness. Perhaps light candles or draw the person's face to have him or her "present." The process is a little like throwing darts at the person's image on a dartboard. Then, in this relaxed ritual space, imagine yourself obtaining the just punishment, much as in a relaxed meditative state (though this experience may feel more intense because you have created this ritual setting).

However, if you do seek mental justice, it's important that you really feel what you are seeking is just, since this gives you the sense of putting things back into balance when you go through the process. After you finish with the visualization, conclude with a reminder to yourself that the situation is *over*. You have done what is necessary to obtain a just result by seeking this mental justice and now you can let the problem bothering you go. It's all behind you, and you can go on to something new.

Overcoming Fears and Inner Conflicts

Sometimes fears and inner conflicts prevent you from expressing what you really want to say or what you mean. This lack of expression can lead you to feel frustrated, resentful, and possibly lead to further miscommunication, all of which will make the conflict even harder to resolve. Accordingly, just as you must learn to deal with your anger, you need to confront any fears or inner conflicts.

These fears might be about almost anything. A fear of failure might prevent you from asking an employer or associate for a raise, a promotion, a chance to take on more responsibility, or other desired perk. Then, because you didn't get what you want, you may feel hostility or anger toward this person, poisoning your future interactions. So you act with reserve or perhaps try to justify your actions by telling yourself that this person is unfair, doesn't like you, is your enemy, or whatever. But underneath this apparent reality is the true but buried reason for the disturbed relationship—your own fear of failure. Thus, not asking for what you want can lead you to relate to the person you fear to ask in ways that bring about the very failure you fear.

Other fears that may hold you back include a fear of ridicule, a fear of wasting time, or a fear of not being as powerful as you should be. It doesn't matter what the particular fear is. The key to overcoming any fears is first to recognize them. Then, decide if the fears are rational in light of the situation. Ideally, you can work on eliminating the fears, so you can act without fear and clear the way to a resolution.

Recognizing Your Fear Barriers

If you aren't clear what your fears are in a conflict, one way to find out is to ask yourself through visualization, which can enable you to tap into the fears not immediately evident to you. It is a powerful technique, enabling you to see how your fears stand in your way.

Begin by relaxing. Get comfortable—sitting or lying down is fine—and focus on your breathing. Breathe in and out deeply five or more times, so you open yourself to an altered state of consciousness. Slowly put up a screen in your mind and see the conflict you want to resolve on the screen before you. See yourself and others involved in some scenes where you are in conflict. The process is like watching different takes or scenes for a movie. Imagine the lights flickering, and see the fast cuts from one scene or frame to another. You are operating the projector and can fast forward from one scene to another. You can focus on a single scene or collage of scenes.

Allow yourself a few minutes for this, so you have a clear sense of what the conflict is about. Then ask yourself what fears are getting in the way of a resolution, and watch the screen for your answers. Don't try to answer this question logically. Try to be as passive and receptive as you can be. Wait for the answer to appear on the screen; don't try to force it. This passive, receptive role frees your inner self or unconsciousness to speak to you. As many artists and writers have found, your unconscious commonly has the answer to a problem your conscious mind can't solve.

You may get this answer in the form of words, or it may come as a picture of your fear. You might even get your answer as more of a feeling. For example, a comfortable, warming glow might be a sign you are attracted to taking a particular action. Alternatively, a tightening pressure in your stomach could be a sign you are resisting a particular event or person.

Determining If Your Fears Are Rational

How rational are your fears? You might be able to tell by thinking about whether the fear you have identified is realistic. It might be—but it might also result from a personal block, such as a lack of self-confidence or feelings of low self-esteem.

For example, you might be resentful because you think your boss won't give you the promotion you feel you deserve. But maybe you're feeling extra anxious because you want the position so much, are afraid you won't measure up, and are projecting your self-doubts onto others, since they're easier to blame than yourself. Asking yourself questions about the reasons for your fears can bring an accurate answer to light. You might also try imagining someone in your situation describing what is going on as a way to distance yourself from the situation, so you get a more objective view. Then, as this outside observer, ask yourself: "What do you think is going on? What would you advise this other person in your role to do?" It's easier to gain perspective when you see things from the outside.

Another approach is to confide in someone else and ask their opinion. Perhaps describe the situation as something that has happened to someone else, such as a friend or co-worker. This way, you can present the story more neutrally, and the person you tell is more likely to give you their honest assessment, rather than telling you something they think you want to hear.

However you arrive at your answer, and whichever it is—a real, externally-based fear or a self-created one—you can now work on overcoming it. Suppose that your boss *doesn't* like you, as you fear; think about what you can do to change this person's opinion so he or she won't stand in your way. Or if you realize you are creating the fear because of your lack of self-confidence, work on improving your self-esteem. The solutions aren't always easy or evident. But knowing where the problem lies enables you to direct your energy efficiently.

Eliminating Your Fears

Once you have identified your fears, your goal is to get rid of any fears in your way of overcoming the conflict or otherwise getting what you want. Once again, the visualization process can help you.

Again, get into a relaxed state and close your eyes. Breathe deeply in and out, and feel the tension slip away. When you feel very relaxed and ready, put your screen back up—you might even see yourself in the theater. Now project an image of your fear onto the screen. Ask for a concrete picture, feeling, or words to appear to represent this fear.

Once you get some response, ask yourself what is the *source* of the fear. Then wait for your response once more. Again, it may be in the form of pictures, feelings, or words.

Take a minute or so to see, hear, or experience this fear and its source on the screen before you. Notice the situations in which this fear arises—you might project several scenes onto your screen. Try to determine the ways in which your fear contributes to the conflict you have with this other person or persons.

Now ask what you can do to get rid of this fear. Again, don't try to answer the question consciously. Just let the answer appear on the screen and notice what it tells you to do. Maybe you'll find that relaxing and not worrying is the answer; that if you're patient, what you fear will go away. Or maybe you'll find you can follow a series of steps to get rid of the fear, such as taking classes to learn the skills that will make you feel more comfortable and competent doing whatever you are doing.

Finally, conclude the visualization with an experience of the fear becoming smaller and vanishing. Use whatever image you like for this. See yourself shooting a laser gun at your fear image, so your fears explode in space. Perhaps see the image of your fears grow smaller and smaller until they become a point of light and finally vanish. Maybe imagine yourself grabbing your fear image like a piece of paper, tearing it up into little bits, and burning it. Or create some image of your own that makes you think of things ending or being destroyed.

Once you've achieved a feeling of completion that your fear is gone, come back slowly into your normal state of consciousness. You should now feel more powerful and better able to deal with your conflict.

In some cases, a single visualization may be all you need. You identify the problem and eliminate it. But in other cases, you may find the fear has been unaffected or is only reduced a little or for a short time. This limited effect is perfectly natural, since your fear may have built up over many years, or you may hold onto it more intensely than you guessed; it can take time to truly reduce or dislodge it. If this is the case, repeat the process from time to time for reinforcement. This repetition is particularly helpful right before you encounter the person with whom you are involved in the conflict. And be sure to follow any steps the visualization suggests to you, such as taking classes or being more assertive.

Another way to eliminate a fear is to confront it head-on and push right through it. To do so, force yourself to do something that frightens you (such as asserting yourself to say what you really want to someone), and experience and acknowledge the fear while you are doing it. It is best to do this gradually, so you confront the fear in a small dose, and slowly work up to confronting something that seems more risky or scary to you. For example, you might start by asserting yourself to a clerk in a store and several sessions later, end up asking your boss for that raise. This way you gradually increase the level of fear you experience and master each new level. It's an approach that psychologists have used effectively in treating people with all sorts of phobias.

You might also combine this confronting your fears method with a visualization. To do so watch yourself go through the steps where you gradually approach your fears and see yourself succeed. If you can visualize this encounter, it gives you the message that your fear is unnecessary, making it easier to let go of that fear. For further reinforcement, repeat the process and us different types of visualizations to destroy any remaining fear, such as laser-zapping the image of your fear, crumpling it up, or throwing it away. It may take some repetition to let a fear go entirely, especially if it is a strong, habitual one. But each time you confront the fear or visualize yourself confronting it, you reduce the fear's charge and hold on you. Ultimately, you will neutralized it.

Affirm Your Fear Is Gone and Congratulate Yourself

Since it is a noteworthy achievement to overcome the fears holding you back, be proud of your courage in doing this, and when you succeed, congratulate yourself.

You might even take a few minutes to visualize yourself fear-free and getting a reward for it. Get into a relaxed state as before. Then, on the screen before you, see yourself engaging in some activity that shows the fear is gone. Say you used to be afraid of speaking openly to your boss; see yourself giving your opinion on something you'd like to see changed at work with complete confidence. Then, see your boss responding thoughtfully and positively in response to your communication.

Reward yourself for your accomplishment, too, by imagining yourself getting something you find rewarding. It could be a reward related to a particular situation you have overcome (such as your boss giving you a medal for calling attention to problems at work, along with a large bonus check). Or you could imagine yourself getting a more general type of reward (such as standing in front of a large cheering audience, receiving a plaque of recognition, or being on a big, all expenses-paid vacation, sipping a piña colada under a palm tree).

After you reward yourself in visualization, return to everyday consciousness feeling good and very proud of your accomplishments. You have overcome a fear and eliminated one more barrier to resolving the conflicts in your life. You have also demonstrated strength and control over your thoughts and feelings.

Applying This Process to Other Negative Feelings

You can use the same visualization and confrontation methods for dealing with other inner conflicts or negative feelings that might contribute to a conflict. For example, if you are feeling guilty, resentful, jealous, or whatever your feeling may be, begin by acknowledging that feeling. Then determine the *source* of the feeling and ask yourself if it is a rational response to an existing situation or if it is generated by your misperceptions.

To successfully deal with outside conflicts, it helps to overcome your inner conflicts or negative feelings, no matter where they come from. Visualization can help you do this, and so can confronting your fears by experiencing the situation in real life. Or perhaps a combination of visualization and confrontation will help. Or try a more gradual confrontation approach where you gradually increase the fear level to confront things that are increasingly difficult for you. Or see yourself in a situation where you have overcome a past conflict to help you feel more confident you can do the same now. Once you succeed in overcoming a particular inner conflict or negative feeling, affirm, acknowledge, and reward yourself for this achievement. Recognize that you have moved past one more barrier, and are now better able to deal with conflicts in the future, and to have better relationships with others and yourself.

7 Avoiding the Responsibility Trap

Responsibility can play a role in conflict in a number of ways. Just as failing to take responsibility can trigger a conflict, so can taking on too much. And trying to make someone else take on responsibility he or she doesn't want can trigger a conflict, too.

These extremes in taking or giving responsibility can produce conflict because of the reaction they produce in others. When one person fails to take responsibility, others can resent being left with the blame or the work. When someone takes on too much responsibility (and perhaps too much of the credit), others can feel resentful or alienated. And no one likes being held responsible for something he or she didn't do.

Often such failures of giving away or taking on too much responsibility occur because of emotional needs, such as a desire to be in control, or conversely, a desire for others to take charge. Another reason is mutual misunderstandings that occur when the parties think they are behaving appropriately from their interpretation of the situation, but the other party responds to their actions in unexpected ways due to a different interpretation. The result? An uproar when people with differing views accuse each other of not being responsible or of taking too much control.

Whatever the reason for the disconnect in taking the expected or desired responsibility, when this happens, people have fallen into the Responsibility Trap. To get out, they have to align their interpretations and perspectives or bring the misunderstandings to the surface to work out a compromise. Following are some examples of different ways to fall into this trap.

The Problem of Not Taking Responsibility

An example of a conflict due to not taking responsibility is a feud that developed between two neighbors, when one neighbor wouldn't take responsibility for the damage she caused her neighbor and blamed her instead.

The problem: Mrs. Ortega had a beautiful oak that grew so big that its spreading branches dropped leaves next door, which clogged up her neighbor Mrs. Warren's drains and then poked a hole in her roof. This let in the rain and cost Mrs. Warren $1,400 to fix. Though both women had lived peacefully in their quiet neighborhood for fifteen years, their anger now was at a boiling point. In the past, Mrs. Ortega had found a few tenants to trim the tree's branches, but now Mrs. Warren felt she wasn't doing enough. Mrs. Ortega felt she had done what she could and couldn't satisfy Mrs. Warren, aside from taking down the tree, which she didn't want to do and felt she couldn't afford to do.

When the two women showed up at a community resolution group meeting, the women were ready to go to court after not being able to come to a firm resolution themselves. Mrs. Warren complained that though Mrs. Ortega had promised to check with her insurance company about the damages and arrange for someone to take away the branches, it didn't happen. But Mrs. Ortega didn't want to admit any of the tree damage was her fault, regardless of what any insurance company or lawyer might say. She felt she had already done what she could to help, had no money to pay for the tree problem, and felt Mrs. Warren was picking on her because she was the only Hispanic on the block. She felt Mrs. Warren was using the tree as an excuse to get money from her to repair her old house and was a hard-to-please, picky person.

The debate went on and on. Mrs. Warren kept trying to bring the discussion back to Mrs. Ortega's responsibility for the tree and its damage, noting that her insurance company had refused to pay because Mrs. Ortega's tree had caused the damage, and she emphasized that she could easily get a lien on Mrs. Ortega's house if she got a judgment. But Mrs. Ortega simply presented herself as a poor, misunderstood old woman with no control over what had happened, since she "didn't plant the tree."

As she argued:

The tree was there when I moved in . . . I don't see how the tree could have caused all the damage to her roof. Her house is old, and there would be damage anyway. She's just trying to get money from me to fix her house . . .

The other neighbors don't have any problem with the tree. They've never complained. Just Mrs. Warren . . . She's very hard to please . . .

I did cut the branches in the past . . . I've tried to be friendly with her, but she doesn't answer . . . I think it's because I'm Spanish . . . So why should Mrs. Warren be so bothered by all this? If I was in her position, I would simply go and fix up my house myself. She certainly knows people who can do that. I wouldn't go out and bother my neighbor and get her involved.

Although Mrs. Warren was so frustrated that she was ready to leave in the middle of Mrs. Ortega's speech and go to her lawyer, some conflict resolution panelists persuaded her to stay, since she had already invested so much time dealing with the issue. Reluctantly she returned, and the group finally managed to hammer out an agreement in which Mrs. Ortega agreed to do certain things, even though she never openly accepted her responsibility. She said she would ask the men in her house to trim the tree and she would ask Legal Assistance to the Elderly for their help with some funds, while Mrs. Warren agreed to supervise the trimming and to ask her own insurance company for reimbursement if Mrs. Ortega couldn't get funds from her insurance or legal aid.

But then, just as the two were on the verge of signing the agreement, everything broke down when Mrs. Ortega began explaining again why she wasn't responsible. Though she seemed willing to sign, she unleashed a torrent of angry words, accusing Mrs. Warren of lying to get her to pay for fixing her house and concluding with these words: "She keeps saying my tree caused the damage, but it didn't. I don't care how many pieces of paper she waves."

And with this Mrs. Warren walked out, since she saw that Mrs.

Ortega was still blaming her and not acknowledging her own responsibility for anything. Any agreement to act would be a fraud. If Mrs. Ortega wouldn't accept her own responsibility and acknowledge the damages her tree caused, Mrs. Warren felt there was no basis for any agreement. So she planned to return to her original plan to take the matter to court, with the result that Mrs. Ortega would face an almost certain judgment against her and a lien on—and possible sale of—her house, since she had no money to pay.

This situation illustrates how failing to take responsibility when one is in the wrong can lead to an impasse in resolving a conflict. This can be hard to do, since taking responsibility means the person has to make amends to fix what is wrong, commonly by paying to fix it or doing extra work. But by not taking responsibility, the person is apt to pay more in the long run, as well as suffer broken relationships and legal problems that could force taking on responsibility anyway. By contrast, if a person accepts responsibility for what he or she has done, he or she can do so in a way that saves face and this provides a basis for resolving a conflict.

Some conflicts can be resolved without trying to assign blame (which may only serve to fan the conflict fires), such as by simply forgiving past wrongs and moving on. But this is not possible when the issue of taking responsibility is a critical issue in the conflict or when one person needs to be compensated for damages. In such situations, it is important for the person causing the damage to acknowledge it. Otherwise, as in Mrs. Warren's case, the person who suffered damage can feel taken advantage of and a mutual agreement becomes almost impossible. The standoff caused by the party at fault not taking responsibility will breed more hostility, and ultimately the person causing the damage may have to pay more. An original refusal to accept a part in doing wrong both prolongs and intensifies a conflict.

What You Can Do

If you find yourself in such a situation and you have some responsibility for what happened, acknowledge it. Let the other person know exactly what you did, from your perspective. This sets a tone of honesty and shows you sincerely want to set things straight. It also allows you to apologize, if you feel that's appropriate. Or you can explain or justify your actions, if the accusations against you seem hostile or unjust, such as by admitting you made a mistake, neglected to do something, or set the wrong priorities. This way, you own up to whatever happened.

At the same time, you don't want to appear too defensive or apologetic, which can feel demeaning and can antagonize the other person by creating an awkward, embarrassing situation. Your emphasis should be speaking honestly about the situation and owning up to what you did or didn't do. In turn, the other person will generally be appreciative, since you are acting in a mature, responsible way.

If you are accused of something you feel you haven't done, try first to understand why you *seem* responsible. Is it possible you are more at fault than you realize, and like Mrs. Ortega, you're trying to deny your responsibility because you can't see the situation objectively or fear the consequences of accepting responsibility?

Also, recognize the difference between taking an action and achieving effective results. Mrs. Ortega did the former when she repeatedly described all her efforts to solve the tree problem (even though they didn't work out), hoping thereby to relieve herself of any further responsibility. But she didn't realize that her responsibility lay in producing *effective results* to resolve the problem; just spending ineffective time trying to achieve that result wasn't enough. Mrs. Warren tried to reasonably hold her to this results-oriented measure but Mrs. Ortega didn't accept this appropriate measure of responsibility—producing results, not just engaging in actions. Mrs. Warren got madder and madder, realizing there was no basis for agreement, since Mrs. Ortega continued to deny her responsibility.

When you are accused of shirking responsibility, look closely and objectively at your role in what happened. Maybe you do need to acknowledge responsibility, although you can do so in a comfortable, positive way (such as by explaining your reasons or higher priorities). Also, you may need to *do* something to work out a fair solution to the conflict. And so you might more comfortably do this, while you edge towards taking responsibility, by taking a hypothetical approach, such as: "Let's say I am responsible. How do you feel we might work out the conflict?" Then, using the "if" approach, you can feel safer as you work out a resolution, without making yourself more vulnerable in a lawsuit if you can't work out a fair resolution. At least show you are willing to take responsibility if you are responsible, since it's better to resolve a conflict before it gets to the lawsuit stage, which will be a more costly way of forcing you to take that responsibility if warranted.

What if someone else is evading the responsibility, and you feel he or she must accept blame to attain a fair solution? Try gently pointing that out, without accusing or blaming the person, urging him or her to recognize and take responsibility for a specific action or failure to act. While an objective approach is best, sometimes people resist seeing things clearly. In that case, try using "I" statements instead of "you" statements in calling attention to what you see.

For instance, after Mrs. Warren found it didn't work to tell Mrs. Ortega repeatedly that her tree was causing damage and she was responsible for doing something about it, she might have confronted her neighbor's failure directly by saying something like: "I feel like you are not willing to recognize that you are responsible for this tree because you are concerned about the costs of this responsibility. I'd like to try to work something out without having to go to court. But the only way I can do this is if you understand you have some responsibility for this. Then we can work on resolving the problem together."

These statements get the real issue on the table: a person's resistance to working out a fair solution, which provides a foundation on which to work on resolving the problem. If not, you may end up going round and round like Mrs. Ortega and Mrs. Warren. Since Mrs. Warren never directly raised the failure-to-take-responsibility issue, Mrs. Ortega never realized that Mrs. Warren understood her reluctance to acknowledge responsibility.

The Problem of Taking Too Much Responsibility

The opposite problem, when someone takes on too much responsibility or tries to, can also be a major source of conflict, leaving others feeling overly controlled or diminished because someone doesn't trust them to do something. In effect, the person taking on the extra responsibility exerts power over the person giving up responsibility, and this action can create even more tension when the person giving up responsibility does so reluctantly or unwillingly. The result is that he or she is likely to feel lowered self-esteem and resentment against the person wielding power. These feelings of hostility might simmer under the surface, held back in the face of the person exercising power. But they can readily erupt into conflict when a situation occurs that fans the flames.

Often the person taking on the extra responsibility can feel angry and resentful too, since having greater responsibility can be an unwanted burden. Someone might feel driven to take on responsibility if it seems the other person won't take it or won't take it competently. Or perhaps one person wants the power and control that comes with being in charge, but doesn't like the additional commitment of time, energy, and effort to exercise that added responsibility.

So both parties can suffer when responsibility is delegated unevenly, and when the controlled party's feelings of resentment, frustration, and tension boil over and the controlling party can no longer hold back those feelings, there can be an overt blowup. It's a pattern that typifies one of the most basic human relationships—that between the parent and child. But when adults are involved, the person pushed into the "child" role by the person trying to act like the responsible "parent" may not like this and may seethe inside or eventually rebel.

The Parent-Child Pattern

It's natural for a parent to do things, give advice, and make decisions for a child, since a child relies on the parent for guidance and protection. But as the child grows, so does the need to assume some of their *own* responsibility and direction. Some parents, however, find it hard to give up control. So a child's anger, confusion, or resentment can grow, because he or she wants to take on more responsibility, but the parents won't allow it.

Angie and her mother developed such a problem, beginning when Angie was still a young child and becoming worse as she grew up. Mother and daughter had frequent screaming battles, separated by uneasy truces until the next battle erupted. The problem for Angie was that her mother said "You can't [or won't] do this" to most things Angie felt able and eager to do. As Angie commented at a workshop, in thinking back to those tumultuous times:

> My mother always wanted to be in charge and tell me what to do, and I resented it. I felt like she was continuing to treat me like a child. She didn't trust me to grow up, even when I was seventeen and eighteen.

> When we went someplace, she would tell me what to wear. If I wanted to choose something I liked, she would argue that I didn't look right or that was trying to wear it to displease her. She was also continually reminding me to do things I already planned to do, like go to an appointment in

school. If I told her she didn't need to remind me, that I could think of these things myself, she would tell me she was just trying to be helpful because I didn't always remember things. She thought I couldn't be responsible but never let me prove I could be.

She was always giving me advice about things when I didn't want her advice, telling me it was for my own good. She would tell me what she thought about my friends, what I should do with my hair, and on and on.

Most of the time, I did what she said to keep the peace. But I kept steaming inside, because I felt she was trying to take over my life. Then, she would push one of my buttons and I would explode, such as giving me still another piece of unwanted advice about my hair or clothes or even something small like how to do the laundry. Then I'd start screaming at her, "No, leave me alone," and she would scream back, "You don't appreciate all I'm trying to do for you." And then when I'd tell her to get off my case, that just made her even madder. These arguments often ended with me storming off and slamming my door, or sometimes I got so tired of all the yelling that I gave in.

However it ended, I usually felt bad and this tension between my mother and me would simmer for days, until we ended up having some battle again.

Though these tensions and battles also upset Angie's mother, Alice, she kept on pushing, because she was concerned her daughter would fare less well without her guidance. Additionally, her own feelings of low self-esteem led her to want to feel control over the situation. Although Angie continually resisted and resented Alice's advice, Alice couldn't help it. She felt driven to speak her mind and couldn't control herself, even when she realized that certain comments were likely to set Angie off. She felt it worth risking an argument to keep Angie's life on track, and wished for a loving, warm mother-daughter relationship, even as her actions were driving Angie away.

The first step toward a solution was taking a long, hard, objective look at the situation, which was spiraling into a state of continued war where the mother and daughter hardly spoke to each other without fighting. Alice realized that she had to change her need to control everything to benefit the relationship. So with the help of some outside advice and a visualization technique to envision a possible future, she decided to risk giving up some of her control to let Angie take more responsibility. She invited Angie to make all the arrangements for a day in the city with some visiting relatives, a visit Angie was already dreading because she could imagine her mother planning every hour of their time together. But then she was pleasantly surprised when her mother suggested that she take charge of the plans.

Though they both were a little nervous—Angie because this was something new, Alice because she worried about something going wrong—the day in the city worked out wonderfully. Angie showed she could plan well, while Alice was able to hold back from interfering and trying to take the reins. Mother and daughter even had a long, honest talk afterwards. Alice acknowledged Angie's success and agreed to give her more space to run her life in the future.

It wasn't easy for Alice, since he had to continually remind herself to give up control. But with the help of counseling, Alice was able to work things out. She learned to hold back her desire to take on responsibility immediately, give advice, and exercise control. She was there if her daughter needed her, but tried to stand back. She learned to let go, and the result was an immediate easing of tensions with her daughter. Alice soon felt a sense of peace and harmony for herself. She was proud of the improved relationship with Angie and proud that Angie could be so responsible. Angie made some poor choices now and then (as everyone does occasionally), but she learned from her errors, as most people do. And Alice replaced her need to exercise control over those who didn't want it by taking on responsibility in volunteer activities, where people appreciated her efforts and were delighted by the responsibilities she took on.

Common Situations Involving Taking On Too Much Responsibility

Any situation where one person takes on too much responsibility can lead to conflicts. These troubled relationships fall into typical patterns.

In one common situation, a person takes on extra responsibility because he or she doesn't think the other person is taking on enough. The other person is often unaware of the need for that responsibility, may have different priorities, or may not be aware of what has to be done since the first person is doing it. For example:

*   *In a conflict between a husband and wife,* the wife thinks the husband should do certain household tasks such as making repairs or clean-

ing up, but the husband doesn't take on these responsibilities, because he is busy doing other things, says he'll get around to them later, or has a different standard of neatness, so he doesn't think performing these tasks is necessary. A classic outcome is that the party who wants the tasks done, the wife in this case, will do them but feel resentful. Or she'll nag her husband to do them, because she feels he should do so. Then, *both* parties will feel put upon. The wife will resent doing the task or having to nag and plead, and the husband will resent time spent inconveniently (or unnecessarily) doing the task or being made to feel bad about not doing it.

- *In a conflict between co-workers on a joint project,* one worker may begin to take over, to the other's dismay. Sometimes he may not really want to do this but does anyway, feeling some need to step in, say because he has certain ideas about how to do the project or doesn't think the other can or will carry it out the work as well. Then, as he takes the lead, he may resent the co-worker for not doing enough, while the co-worker may feel shut out of the process or that he has lost control over it. And he is likely to resent the other person, too, for pressing ahead.

A key problem in both these situations is that the person taking on the extra responsibility may be able to accomplish the goal more efficiently alone or by directing both people's actions. But the costs of such an action may often outweigh the benefits, because feelings of anger and resentment can simmer or erupt on both sides. The person taking on the responsibility can feel burdened by the extra work and feel alone. Meanwhile, the person turning over the responsibility can feel a lowered sense of self-esteem, as well as an uncomfortable dependence and a loss of individuality. Also, hostile feelings may readily expand into full-blown conflict. And even if such feelings remain unshared under the surface, their toll in stress, anger, suspicion, and paranoia can be high.

Getting Out of the Responsibility Trap

You can fall into the responsibility trap from different angles, and land on different sides of it. One side is a perceived problem with *you:* you seem to be taking on too much responsibility or not as much as others would like. The other side is a perceived problem with another person:

that person seems to you to be taking too much control over a situation or not taking as much as he or she should.

The two sides of the problem are like the opposite ends of a teeter-totter or seesaw. You take on too much responsibility if the other person leaves too much up to you, and vice versa, with the responsibility taken by one party increasing as the responsibility taken by the other declines. So the key to resolving the problem is to figure out how most appropriately and comfortably to reapportion the responsibility. This way you resolve the problem for the future, regardless of who is to blame for taking on or not taking on enough responsibility in the present or past. The matrix of the responsibility trap will look something like this:

Amount of Responsibility Assumed

	Too Much	Too Little
Self		
Other		

Party Taking On Responsibility Role

The first step to getting out of the trap is to look more closely at the situation, putting aside any strong feelings you might have developed about who's at fault and who isn't, even if the conflict has become a recurring pattern. Don't let your emotions rule. Instead, check out the accuracy of your perceptions and consider the other's view of you. Also consider possible reasons for either side to take on or avoid certain responsibilities.

One way to check the accuracy of each other's perceptions is to share your view of the situation with each other. This sharing could raise some tensions, so preface this sharing with an agreement that you will each listen to the other with respect and attention, even though you might each hear things you don't agree with. Then, after one person has finished, the other can respond by correcting or verifying any perceptions and possibly providing an explanation for why such and such occurred. Another possibility is for you both to engage in a role-play in which you each imagine what the situation may have looked like from the other's eyes.

Alternatively, if your feelings are still too tense for a direct discussion or role-play to be comfortable, suggest that each of you put your feelings and perceptions of the situation in a letter to each other. Then, after you both review these letters, meet to have a discussion. The process of writing and exchanging such letters can help clarify issues and provide explanations. This writing can also help to release feelings and calm everyone down to pave the way for a fruitful discussion and an exchange of views.

If at any time in the course of this analysis you realize you were doing or denying something that contributed to the conflict, acknowledge that to yourself. You need this initial self-awareness to decide how to deal with the situation. It can also help to acknowledge this to the other person to show your good faith in taking on responsibility where it's due.

What to Do When You Are Accused of Not Doing Enough

Suppose you have been in a conflict with a significant other or co-worker who blames you for not doing certain tasks. You have been getting increasingly angry at that person for bugging you about this. If it's so important to him, you think, why doesn't he do it himself? But he thinks you should do it, and so the conflict continues.

To start the resolution process, look first at what the person is claiming about you. Could it be accurate? If not, correct any faulty assumptions. Or the claims may be misplaced because of a lack of clarity about who should do what. If so, discuss roles and responsibilities openly. Alternatively, if the person's perception is accurate, consider why you might be avoiding that responsibility. Maybe you don't like doing the task, don't think it is necessary, have different ideas about the value of doing it, feel the other person isn't doing enough in other areas, or feel you should get more pay or recognition for doing more.

Whatever the reasons for the conflict over taking responsibility, the point is to understand what is causing the other person to view your actions in a certain way. Are your actions or your perceptions at fault, or are the other person's perceptions? And why are you choosing to act as you do in taking on or avoiding certain responsibilities? You need to clarify your understanding of what's going on before you can decide what is the best way for you to deal with the conflict.

When you do examine what's causing the conflict, you may decide that taking on the role the other person wants you to perform isn't such a big deal and that you're willing to give in and do more—an example of *accommodating*. Or you may want to stand up for what you are doing and get the other person to back down, if you feel the other person is making unfair claims on your time—an example of taking a more *competitive/confrontational* approach. Or perhaps you might suggest a *compromise*, where you take on more responsibility in this area to please the other, but ask him or her to do something you want in return. Finally, if it's worth the time and effort to discuss the situation in depth, you might be able to *collaborate* with the other party to find an alternative solution.

Whatever approach you ultimately decide is most suitable for this particular situation, you should base your choice on your most important goals and priorities, based on a clear appraisal of the situation.

What to Do When You Feel the Other Person Isn't Doing Enough

Conversely, if you are in a situation where you feel the other person isn't doing enough, first consider whether your own perceptions are accurate. Can you think of any reasons he or she might have to avoid this responsibility? These considerations will give you some basis for proposing or discussing possible solutions.

For example, if an associate hasn't done something, and you have been nagging her to do it, try writing down a list of possible explanations for her behavior: she doesn't like it; doesn't think she can do it well; feels you should do it yourself; or doesn't find it worthy of her time and attention. Then, consider which of these explanations is most likely in terms of her personality and past behavior.

Once you have a sense of the other person's reasons, you can tailor a discussion to address *her* needs as well as your own. Be sure to treat your assessment as an educated, reasoned guess, which you still have to check out to determine if it's correct. Before you do bring up the subject, consider how important this responsibility is for you. It may be that you'd rather quickly perform the action yourself. Or if you do want the other to do it, a clearer awareness of what both you and your associate need might enable you to work out an agreement for the other to do it, in return for a compromise offer from you. If the task doesn't seem important to her, for instance, you might assure her that it is important to *you*, and offer to do something she values in return. For example:

If your employee will come in over the weekend to do a crucial unexpected project for you . . .	You will let your employee take off an extra Friday to have a long weekend anytime next month.
If your roommate will agree to turn off the stereo at 10:00 p.m. . . .	You will agree to be quiet in the morning and you will take your usual shower later in the day.
If your friend will agree to walk the dogs both mornings and evenings this week . . .	You will go to that luncheon with your friend, although you really would rather not.

What to Do if One Person Is Doing Too Much

The same analytic process can be used to consider a situation where one person is taking on too much responsibility and denying the other person power. Ask yourself whether either of you is doing too much. Consider the possible reasons causing this, such as:

- You don't trust the other person to do it right—or he doesn't trust you.
- You want to prove your worth by showing how much you can do—or the other person is seeking such validation.
- One of you likes the feeling of power and control.

Which possibility sounds most plausible to you? Assess your own and the other person's likely priorities, and your answers should suggest ways of resolving the conflict.

What to Do if You Are Doing Too Much

For example, if you realize you *are* doing too much and are undermining the other person's self-esteem, resulting in hostility and resentment, maybe it's time to do a little less and let go. Some possibilities might be:

- Discuss what the other person needs to do so you will feel comfortable letting go. This way if you agree to give away some responsibility, you can make it clear that you need to feel the other person will act responsibly in return. Then if the other person agrees, allow him the space to do so.

- Acknowledge and support the person in other ways, so you can continue doing what you are doing. Perhaps verbal praise and recognition for roles already filled is enough.

- Show the person some techniques so he knows what to do.

The best approach depends on the situation and the needs, interests, and priorities you each bring to the situation.

What to Do if You Feel the Other Person Is Doing Too Much

If the other person is taking on too much responsibility from your point of view, use the same process in reverse. Start by examining the reality of your perceptions, and imagine *why* the other person might be doing this. Then, act accordingly. Some possibilities might be:

- If doing so much is really important to the other person, you might work on calming and relaxing yourself, so his or her actions don't make you so resentful. Allow yourself to let go if you can, and if it's worth keeping the peace.

- If the other person needs some help, which he or she hasn't asked for, offer to do more yourself. For example, suggest that you could do some task because you know the person is very busy, and this could give him or her more time for other things.

- If the other person is doing the work because he or she distrusts you to do it properly, point out that you would like to learn how to do something, so you can do it well. Maybe write up a note with your suggestions on how a particular task might be done and what you can contribute—an especially good approach in a work situation if you have an insecure boss who is afraid to give up responsibility because he isn't sure the employees are up to it.

Again, the particular approach depends on the circumstances and what you and the other person most want.

Putting It All Together

The responsibility trap can cause a great deal of tension between people when they have different ideas about who should do what and different priorities about what they want to do. Whatever the situation, the way to get out of the trap is to look more closely at your own and the other's perceptions, priorities, and rationales for acting more or less responsibly.

Based on what you find and the importance of the issue to you and the other party, you can choose your solution:

- Find ways to step away from the situation (avoiding).
- Relax or accommodate yourself to what the other party wants to do (accommodating).
- Work out a compromise (compromising).
- Deal with the problem at length to find a joint solution (collaborating).
- Continue doing what you are doing, while finding a way to make the other person feel better about the situation (delaying decision making).

The chart on page 92 can help you in deciding what kind of approach to use.

1. Is it true?

2a. If so, why? What are the reasons? Lack of trust? The issue isn't important? Other?

2b. If not, why not? Are there incorrect perceptions? Are there wrong assumptions? Different priorities?

3a. What can you do to straighten things out? If lack of trust, build trust. If not important enough, let the other person do it. If too important to risk not doing it, do it yourself.

3b. What can you do to straighten things out? If incorrect perceptions, correct them. If wrong assumptions, bring errors into the open and change your assumptions. If different priorities, work out compromise so both achieve the best solution possible.

Understanding the Responsibility Trap and Figuring How to Get Out

What is the problem? You claim the other party is taking:

		Too Little Responsibiliy	Too Much Responsibility
The Other Party Claims You Are Taking	**Too Little Responsibiliy**	Conflict over one person doing too much when or because the other is doing too little	Conflict over having control
	Too Much Responsibility	Conflict over no one doing the job	Conflict over one person doing too much when or because the other is doing too little

It's easy to fall into the responsibility trap, and it requires conscious effort to climb out. But once you make the effort, you'll be more wary of such traps in the future. You'll recognize the early danger signs of someone taking on too little or too much responsibility, so you can avoid the trap by keeping responsibilities more evenly balanced or working out agreements so people feel comfortable with an uneven split. You'll avert potential conflicts before they reach full pitch.

Section
Three

Applying Your Reason

8

Overcoming Conflicts Through Better Communication

Communication, the key to resolving most conflicts, is itself often the *cause* of conflict. Any breakdown of communication can lead to conflict. Sometimes one or both parties aren't clear. Sometimes one or both parties aren't listening. Often there are misunderstandings about meanings. Hidden assumptions can stand in the way. And sometimes lack of communication itself results in misunderstandings that lead to hostility or resentment.

But you can harness the power of communication to break these blocks. A little knowledge and practice will help you send out an appropriate message that is accurately heard and returned. Just keep in mind the basic principles of communication.

Many of the communication principles sound like common sense. Even so, people commonly remain unaware of them, making miscommunication—and thus conflict—more likely. In addition, once the emotions are triggered in a conflict it can become difficult to draw consciously on these principles. But if you develop a constant awareness of them, you can avert potential conflicts before they begin or reach full pitch. You'll even be able to respond effectively—and almost instinctively—if you find yourself midbattle.

This chapter highlights these basic principles. As you read through them, notice examples in your everyday life. Spend a day or two paying close attention to people communicating around you, and you're likely to find examples of each typical error. You might then think of ways to correct the error (but it's usually best to keep your awareness to yourself, since others may not appreciate your corrections). The principles and remedies outlined below should help you make these corrections.

The Discrepancy Between Nonverbal and Verbal Communication

Experts in the communication field tell us that we get about 55 percent of our information from the *nonverbal* communication (such as facial gestures and body movements) that accompanies a spoken message. We get about 38 percent from the voice, pitch, tone, and sounds we hear and only 7 percent from content. (Or at least those are the statistics I've heard again and again at workshops.)

Whatever the exact numbers are, the power of nonverbal cues means that we are often likely to misinterpret or discredit the message someone thinks he or she is communicating. We might hear one thing, but if we sense that someone really feels or means something else from his or her nonverbal cues, trust can break down, or we may react negatively or inappropriately. If someone seems nervous, for instance, no matter how cogent the message, we may not believe it. If someone apologizes, but seems hesitant, we may feel he or she is insincere and become even angrier.

Accordingly, if you are speaking and feel a sense of distrust, distance, or negativity growing between you and the other person, pause for a moment or even continue the conversation at another time. Ask yourself if their resistance could be due to a discrepancy between the message you want to convey and the way you are presenting it. Body language is often unwilled—but it can be controlled. Once you are aware of a problem, you can try to bring things back into alignment. For example, act humble if you're apologizing. Look your listener in the eye if your message is especially important one, since eye contact is perceived as a sign of sincerity. You might even mention the lack of alignment you perceive to reassure the other person, such as by saying something like: "I don't feel like I'm getting my message across very well. Can you tell me what's wrong?"

To illustrate how this lack of alignment can poison a relationship, picture a husband and wife having a quarrel because she mistrusts him. He has trouble showing his feelings, so the wife doesn't believe him when he says he loves her. So the words come across as just words and wife imagines the worst—another woman. The husband might be able to short-circuit the conflict by admitting his difficulty in expressing his feelings. He might even admit that he understands her lack of trust because of his failure to convey his sincerity adequately. With this revelation, the wife might better understand the real reason for her mistrust. The conversation becomes more anchored in reality, and this helps to defuse conflict.

Similarly, at work, suspicions can grow when one employee makes what he thinks is a helpful suggestion to another. But the employee receiving the message might perceive that the words are said with a seemingly dismissive tone, so the suggestion sounds like a put-down, as if to say: "You're too stupid to have thought of it, but I know what to do." But if the first employee can show he is really offering the suggestion in a spirit of goodwill then the tension might disappear.

Accordingly, look for any signs your own messages may not be received as intended and seek to clarify them if that's the case. Conversely, if you experience a discrepancy between verbal and nonverbal content of someone else's speech, it might help to bring that out in the open. For example, such a discrepancy might consist of the following out-of-phase words, gestures, tones, or body movements:

- A smile indicating friendliness, but a cold, hostile tone of voice, clenched hands, or a movement away from you, indicating anger or dislike.

- A message proclaiming trust and a close, warm relationship, but a hesitant manner and shifting eye-contact, suggesting a lack of confidence or sincerity.

- An aggressive tone and words of attack, suggesting anger and blame.

You probably have your own directory of what nonverbal body cues mean to you, and a careful study of body language will make you even more aware.

By calling attention to a discrepancy you notice, you can show the person you aren't convinced by what he or she is saying, or you are confused by the difference between what he or she is saying and doing and want to understand what the person really means. Make these points in a nonhostile, nonthreatening way, using a gentle tone of voice to express what you perceive and how you feel. Respectfully request that the other person help you understand, since you really would like to resolve the problem. For instance, say something like: "I feel you might be angry about something because of the tone of your voice, although you say you aren't. If so, can we discuss this, so we can deal with whatever is bothering you?"

Once your perception is out in the open, you give the other person a chance to address any underlying feelings or issues that exist (which is usually the case when you perceive a discrepancy). Then you can both deal directly with this underlying problem fueling the conflict, rather than letting it continue to bubble along under the surface.

The Problem of Hidden or Wrong Assumptions

It's natural to enter any interaction with certain assumptions. You assume a particular approach will work well with someone you know, based on your past experience. You assume that someone will share your kind of humor and understand when you are making a joke. And when you say something, you assume it's heard and understood the way you meant it. Such assumptions come naturally and facilitate the everyday flow of interpersonal reactions. Most of the time these assumptions operate unconsciously, letting you focus on the content of what the other person says or does.

But sometimes assumptions can get you in trouble, such as when your comment hits someone the wrong way, or your joke falls flat, because the other person doesn't share the underlying assumption on which the comment or joke was based. Also, in a more serious situation, you might assume someone has understood, believes in, or has agreed to something, when he or she has not.

Conversely, another person might make similar incorrect assumptions about your beliefs, plans, or reaction to something. Such scenarios can lead to real conflict, all the more upsetting because it's often hard to pin down where the problem started. Whenever something important remains unclear or unsaid, it's easy to fill in the blank with a logical assumption. But since the assumption might be wrong, you need to be cautious about the assumptions you make and ready to modify them if some discrepancy suggests they might be incorrect. Also, you need to be ready to make others aware of their own assumptions (tactfully, of course) when they seem to have incorrect assumptions about you.

In the worst case, mistaken assumptions can become self-fulfilling prophecies, as happened to Jerry, an administrative assistant in a large company. He got the impression that a co-worker Sam didn't like him, because he felt Sam had slighted him one day in the company cafeteria by not returning his greeting. A few days later, when his employer called him on the carpet for making personal calls and using the computer for personal purposes, Jerry suspected that Sam had reported him to his boss. So in turn, he decided to make things difficult for Sam and engaged in some petty sabotage. He failed to give him some messages and gave him others incorrectly. As the sabotage continued, Sam began to experience problems (lost phone numbers, wrong dates), and began to wonder if Jerry was for some reason doing these things intentionally. Sam became increasingly antagonistic toward Jerry, and tensions between the two men built until they led to a name-calling argument, after which the two avoided each other at work. In effect, Jerry's assumptions created the reality he assumed. This situation continued until a mutual friend got the two men to discuss what had happened rationally and restore peace. Only then did Jerry uncover his original wrong assumptions that had escalated into this quarrel—Sam had not been trying to avoid him in the cafeteria; he had simply not seen him, and the boss's confrontation with him was due to the company's new policy of cracking down on the personal use of office equipment; it had nothing to do with his co-worker snitching on him. And fortunately, the boss hadn't been aware of Jerry's childish behavior or he might have fired him, regardless of whether Jerry's assumptions had been true.

All sorts of everyday conflicts can arise out of misplaced assumptions. One person assumes the other will take care of something for a meeting, when the other person assumes the same; the task doesn't get done. A woman suspects a friend of secretly dating her boyfriend when she isn't; as a result, both a friendship and the relationship with the boyfriend are lost. A man blames another for doing something he was *reported* to have done but didn't, and an argument between them turns violent. These faulty assumptions lead not only to conflict but to loss as well.

The best way to deal with such situations based on flawed assumptions is to avoid them by not jumping to conclusions or acting on the faulty assumptions in the first place. Instead, wait to get a confirmation of your initial impressions. Such a preventative strategy can help you avoid the needless worry, anger, and confusion due to taking such ill-founded actions, and from trying to repair the damaged relationships afterwards. Some ways to avoid these problems include the following:

- In an uncertain or unclear interaction, ask yourself what you are assuming. Consider how much of your theory is based on *fact,* and where you are filling in the blanks. If the situation is complex, consider writing down a list of the evidence you have. Then, imagine that you are on an impartial jury listening to this. Would the evidence really convince you? How certain can you really be of your assumptions?

- If you are operating on a tentative theory, try playing the devil's advocate to question it. Consider the possibility of an alternate theory, and ask yourself if the other person's behavior might make sense in that light.

- If you have the slightest doubt about your initial assumption, challenge it by bringing it out in the open. Then, ask clear questions or gather hard evidence to support your theory.

- If possible, share your questionable assumptions with the person who these assumptions are about. Get feedback straight from the source to see if your assumptions are correct. In any case, such openness of discussion can help to clear the air. Whether your assumptions were correct or not, the discussion opens up the door to apologies, new agreements, renewed relationships, and the possibility of change for the better.

Once a conflict has begun because of faulty assumptions, the same principle applies toward finding a remedy, since you may be able to stop the problem by revealing these assumptions. By bringing these assumptions out in the open, you can find out what really is fact and what is not. Go back as far as necessary to get to the bottom of things by asking questions and listening.

In the event you feel the conflict is due to the other person's faulty assumptions, you can use the following techniques to help uncover and change them:

- Ask yourself if you think the other person's behavior or attitude towards you could be based on wrong assumptions about what you think, believe, have done, or will do. Consider if you have done or said anything that might have given rise to the other person's suspicions, mistrust, or lack of correct knowledge about you.

- Suggest to the other person (tactfully again) that you think that some misunderstanding may be contributing to the conflict and that you would like to clear them up. Then, describe what you think the problem or faulty assumption might be and give the other person a chance to react. Be ready to explain, clarify, apologize, or show your willingness to accept the other's explanations, clarifications, or apologies.

- If the other person has made an incorrect judgment, give him or her a way to save face and back off. Your goal should be to get him to give up the wrong assumption, not to prove him wrong. If the person senses that you are trying to prove him at fault, this could lead him to hang on to his wrong assumption to save face.

Thus, the best way to prevent or defuse a conflict is to bring assumptions (whether yours or the other person's) into the open to discuss them. Find out what's true and not true, and smooth over any statements or actions due to these wrong assumptions. For example, when Jerry and his co-worker finally talked about what had happened between them and recognized their false assumptions leading to the conflict, they were able to patch up their relationship. Certainly, you may need to additionally address other difficulties arising from actions taken due to the false assumptions—but getting the assumptions out in the open by talking about them is a start.

The Problem of No Communication

Sometimes even when two people appear to be speaking freely, they may fail to communicate important information or hold back their true feelings, thoughts, or desires. Then, they feel angry or resentful when the other person doesn't give them what they want or acts in ways they don't like. In another scenario, people fail to ask for clarification when they don't understand someone else's communication. But the problem in both cases is a lack of communication, so the other person doesn't know what to do. In short, no communication can lead people to act inappropriately or fail to act, which can contribute to conflict. Then, since resolution rests on communication, the problem escalates as long as the communication remains blocked.

You can see examples of this lack of communication problem all around you. For example, if you look at the advice columns in daily newspapers, you'll see this is a common complaint: "My husband doesn't talk to me . . . he shuts me out of his life . . . he doesn't share his feelings." "My boss is always blaming me for things but doesn't tell me what he wants me to do." "We have relatives who barge in and stay with us for days, and I feel very resentful. I've tried to give them hints that we don't want them there by saying how much work we have with the kids, but still they come each year. What can we do?"

In so many of these cases, the solution seems so obvious—why don't you just tell the person causing the problem what you really think or feel? Don't beat around the bush; don't drop hints and let the other person guess. Just say what you want. Be diplomatic; be tactful. But say it. The neglected wife might point out that she feels shut out and would like to understand and share with her husband. The employee might point out to his boss that he would like clearer instructions. The put-upon wife with relatives might simply tell the relatives that it isn't convenient for them to stay because of the children or they might come another time when she has less work, or perhaps if they come they might help out.

The key to the no-communication problem is, not surprisingly, communication. Be open; talk about whatever is hidden or unclear, and if it's hard to assess those hidden needs, refer back to the discussion in Chapter 5 on recognizing needs and wants. Otherwise, the tensions due to a lack of communication can build into a painful stalemate or displays of resentment or anger. Or you might end up worrying about or reacting to something based on a misperception.

To avoid this no-communication problem, you can do some of the following:

• Ask yourself if you are saying what you mean. Is there anything you are saying that could be unclear or subject to misinterpretation by the other person? You might look for cues that indicate the other person didn't understand you, such as a confused, bewildered look or a repeat of a previous question or conversation. Then, if you think there was a communication misfire, slow down, back up, or explain in other words what you said. Alternatively, ask the other person to state what he or she thinks you said, to see if he or she did understand. If not, you can explain again.

- Ask yourself if you are saying what you really want, need, or feel. If not, you probably won't get what you hope to get. If you are talking about something that is sensitive or unpleasant to deal with, couch it in diplomatic language or build up to it tactfully and gradually. But if you are beating around the bush too much, what you are saying won't be clear. So even if it is difficult for you, zero in on what you really want to say. You might even let the other person know you find it difficult to say this, to prepare the way for your comments.

- Ask yourself if you understand the other person. Are you really listening openly and receptively? Are any of your own assumptions, expectations, needs, or desires getting in the way? If there is any uncertainty, one helpful technique is to describe what you think you heard the other person say. Then, see if he or she agrees. If so, you can move on; if not, ask the person to explain again.

The Problem of Being Unclear

A corollary to the no-communication problem is the problem of being unclear, which can similarly lead to many misunderstandings about what is said or meant. It can be tempting to be vague or unclear if your subject is an uncomfortable one. You may want to skip details if you are pressed for time. You may want to use a smokescreen to avoid taking responsibility. A lack of clarity may also be a useful crutch if you want to fudge your responses, so you have deniability, such as in political discourse.

You can also contribute to the lack of clarity problem as a listener. Some examples are when you feel embarrassed to admit you didn't "get" something or don't want to slow things down or disturb the other person by suggesting something stated is unclear.

Although at times a lack of clarity may prove appealing—even a strategy to help you achieve a goal—ultimately, the failure of communication will make itself felt. A delay in clearing things up can make the situation worse, as more incorrect statements and wrong actions may follow the initial lack of understanding. The spiral of wrongheaded responses and counterresponses can lead you into an escalating spiral of conflict.

A good example of the danger of unclear communication is the boss who asks his or her employee to do something, but gives unclear instructions (or at least the employee doesn't understand them). Then, if the employer doesn't confirm with the employee that the instructions were clearly understood and if the employee doesn't seek clarification—either because he thinks he understands, or doesn't want to admit being unsure about what to do, or is afraid of being criticized for not knowing—the result is a job done wrong! Depending on how seriously wrong it is, the mistake might lead to major conflicts, lost jobs, even lawsuits. In this situation, the fault lies with both the boss, who did not make sure important information is clearly presented and understood, and the employee, who did not ask the boss to explain what he did not understand early on.

Similarly, personal relationships can easily disintegrate into confusion and turn into a conflict when a lack of clarity leads to misunderstandings. For example, Nora told a friend she was arriving at the airport at a certain time and asked her friend to pick her up. She even gave the airline and the flight number. But Nora had forgotten to indicate which airport, so her friend went to the city airport, whereas Nora flew into an airport in a nearby city which she usually used because of less traffic and hassle. Neither thought to ask which airport, since each thought the airport meant was perfectly clear. The women were communicating past each other instead of double-checking what each heard and understood. Are you surprised they ended up angry at one another?

All sorts of everyday—and not so everyday—problems are triggered by unclear communication, such as missed appointments, misquotes in articles and reports, wrong job specs, and rumors based on wrong facts. The list goes on and on.

But again, the solution is simple and obvious. If you hear something and don't understand what the person said, wants, or means, simply say you aren't clear. Even if you *think* you understood, it's a good idea to repeat back what you think the other means to be sure. Don't repeat things continually, since this will bog down the conversation. But when you do repeat back occasionally, this reassures the speaker that you are listening attentively, and serves to show that you understand what was said (or gives the speaker a chance to make corrections if you do not).

And when *you* are giving the instructions, ask the other person to describe briefly what he or she heard you say to be sure what you said was understood. It's especially crucial to do this if the information you conveyed is very important or complex. Make sure that the understandings go both ways. If you do find any misunderstandings in either direction, talk about what is wrong and clarify what is unclear or incorrect. The process may sound very elementary. Yet, often people take it for granted that what they said was clear and understood, and don't think to question whether this was in fact the case. The result is that misunderstandings and conflicts can build—all from a simple communication that turned out to be unclear.

So concentrate on being clear. Spell out what you mean. And look for signs the other person understands what you are saying: such as by responding "I understand" or "I got it," and showing by replies or reactions that he or she *really* got your meaning. If at times you're not sure or the message is very important or complex, ask the person to repeat his understanding of your message to you to make sure he really does understand correctly. And if *you* fail to understand something the first time, admit it. Don't worry about seeming dense or stupid. You only err if you act like you have understood something when you haven't, because then you are likely to make a mistake. By acknowledging when you don't understand something, you're saving face in the long run and showing you are open, forthright, and eager to get things right from the start.

Learning to Listen Well

Just as many people think they are expressing themselves well when they are not, many people don't know how to listen well. So no wonder communication attempts often go awry with communication errors on both sides.

Good or "active" listening is one of the most effective communication skills you can learn. It will help you avoid the problems described in this chapter: acting from wrong assumptions, leaving important information unclear, and failing to communicate entirely.

Failing to listen well is a major source of conflict for reasons other than not getting the correct information. Not listening can convey an impression of hostility, bias, or negative criticism of the person speaking. The body language that accompanies not listening attentively, such as frowns, restlessness, and gestures of impatience, can show a lack of interest, disregard, or empathy. In turn, the speaker is apt to feel disrespected or diminished, which can create a real strain in the relationship, though this effect is entirely unintended by you.

Conversely, if you can make another person feel really listened to, acknowledged, and understood, you'll minimize your chances of conflict and ill will. You'll also profit from whatever information he or she is trying to convey. This doesn't mean you have to agree with everything the person is saying. But the person needs to feel *heard* by having his or her communication accepted. It's the same principle as allowing an angry person to vent feelings as you listen receptively. The ideal is to listen with empathy, so you show that you accept what the person is saying without judgment and understand how he or she might see things, even if you don't see things the same way.

Sometimes it can be hard to adopt this empathetic listener approach, especially in the midst of an upsetting conflict. But if you can calm yourself down enough to concentrate on active listening, you will find that this approach can do wonders for resolving the conflict. It will help to calm the other person if he or she is agitated and upset. It will pave the way for a clearer discussion of the conflict.

According to communications experts, you should listen for two things when you listen attentively:

1. Listen for content—what's actually being said.
2. Listen for feelings—how the person feels about what he or she is saying and about you.

Listening for feelings is especially critical in a conflict situation, since a lot of feelings can be buried under the outward message, and it's essential to bring those feelings out to achieve a satisfying, lasting resolution. Otherwise, unexpressed hostilities can fester, such as in the case of a spouse who finally says "Fine, fine, do that" to end the argument. Yet, he or she is still seething underneath. The external argument may be over, but the internal conflict is ongoing and it will heat up again.

If you are in a situation where someone has underlying negative feelings, the chances are you will sense anger or resentment in the person's voice. You may want to overlook those perceptions to maintain an outward calm. But the best approach is to acknowledge the unvocalized feelings you sense in order to work on clearing the air. One way to do this is to say something to suggest what you think the other person may be feeling underneath, such as: "I sense that . . ." or "It sounds like . . ." Then, add your interpretation: "You may be feeling ———" [and you fill in the blank]. This way, by gently suggesting what you perceive (not by trying to impose your interpretation on the other person with a comment like, "You must be feeling . . ."), the other person knows you are just checking, not presuming, and are concerned to resolve the problem, not just get it out of the way. Then, he or she can let you know if you are correct about these unresolved feelings and will feel heard and understood. Once true feelings are out in the open or consciously set aside after being expressed, you are more likely to achieve a mutual and more deeply satisfying resolution.

For example, if you hear someone say something that suggests he isn't saying what he really means, you might reply with a question or observation that shows your concern and gives the person permission to state his real feelings or concerns. The following chart illustrates how you might interpret and respond to the meanings you sense from what someone says.

What the Person Says	What You Think He or She Means or Feels	What You Might Say to Bring Out the Real Meanings or Feelings
"Do what you want."	"I don't like what you want to do, but I don't feel like you care about what I think. I feel that you are going to do it your way in any event."	"I feel that you may not really want this. What do you *really* want, and can we talk about it?"
"I don't care."	"I do care, but I feel frustrated. You aren't listening to what I am saying."	"But you do seem to be annoyed by what happened, and I'm concerned about how you feel."
"Have it your way."	"I'm too tired to struggle with you anymore. Do what you want, but I don't like it."	"But I'd like to be sure I have your input and agreement, too. What would you like to see happen, so we can both get what we want?"
"Fine" [or any other words of apparent approval that are spoken in a reluctant or angry tone of voice].	"It's not the slightest bit fine, and I'm really very angry with you. I feel like I'm being pushed around."	"But it sounds like it *isn't* fine for you. What do you really feel about this? I'd truly like to know."

Keep in mind that listening for *real* feelings is one of the key principles of listening well. The other principles to follow include:

- *Listen with empathy.* Regardless of how wronged or hostile you feel, disengage from your own feelings and listen with an open, receptive mind. Try to put yourself in the place of the other person. Picture how the situation looks from his or her perspective. Imagine how *you* and your responses sound from the other's point of view.

- *Focus on the issues.* Don't get sidetracked by responding to the person's personality. Remind yourself to listen to what the person is saying about the issues involved in the dispute. If the conversation strays, ask questions to get the conversation back on track.

- *Show positive regard and respect for the other person.* Whatever the person says, remind yourself that you will show respect for what that person is saying and feeling. Likewise, remind yourself that you will not get sucked into name-calling or other shows of disrespect. So if the person says something like: "You really are a jerk," don't escalate the conflict by responding in kind. Instead, respond with understanding and empathy to his or her underlying feelings, such as by acknowledging his or her anger or frustration. Get the discussion back to the issues by saying something like: "It sounds like this situation is really upsetting to you. What would you like to do about it?" Perhaps give a reminder about the need to treat each other with respect by saying something like: "I know you're angry, but let's try not to call each other names, and let's work on solving this problem." In other words, take the high ground as you listen to try to keep the emotions under control. Then, when you can, get back to dealing constructively with the problem.

- *Listen attentively without judgment.* This way you encourage the other person to say what he or she really thinks and express any feelings that might be standing in the way of working out the problem. It allows the other person to "blow off steam." One way to do this nonjudgmental listening is to nod from time to time or offer occasional responses like "uhhuh," or comments like: "Then what happened?" or "How did you feel?" Such gestures and questions show that you're paying attention. They also help create an open, nonjudgmental environment where the other person feels free to express what he or she really thinks. Ideally, by modeling attentive, nonjudgmental listening, you'll encourage the other person to do the same, thereby creating a more receptive environment for jointly reaching a productive solution to the conflict.

- *Reflect back what you think you heard to show the other person you're really listening.* Use your own words to repeat important points the other person is making. You might also share your perceptions of what you think the other person is feeling. This way you are a kind of mirror to the other person, showing you are really listening and understanding. Yet, you are not parroting back the words. You are paraphrasing what the person said, along with presenting your perception of the other's feelings. This process not only shows the other person you are listening, but helps to clarify his or her message in your own mind. It also ensures you're not mishearing, because you give the other person a chance to correct you if you have heard anything wrong.

  In paraphrasing, you might begin by saying something like: "Let me see if I understand what you just said . . ." or "Am I correct in thinking that you're saying . . . ?" Then, restate what you heard in your own words. If you are reflecting the other person's feelings, you might say something like, "You sound _____ [angry, upset, confused] about _____ [identify the situation]." Be careful not to sound too definite or sure of yourself in reading feelings, which projects your assumptions or perceptions on the other person. Instead of saying "You are/must be confused about . . ." say something like: "You *seem* confused about . . ."
  A sympathetic, interpretive comment can be particularly useful when someone is very upset. It helps the other person know his or her emotion has registered with you, even though it was expressed through a confusion of words and feelings. When you say something like: "It looks like you are really angry about that," or "It seems like that experience was really painful for you," assuming your perception is reasonably accurate, the other person can feel your concern and understanding. It may even help the person clarify his own uncertain feelings. That helps break down communication barriers.

- *Clarify what you don't understand or are unsure about.* This way you know what's going on. The key here is to get more information if you don't understand or are uncertain about what the other person really means or feels. This principle may sound obvious, but often people go on in conversations without filling in these gaps. Then misunderstandings can build and build. For instance, say things like: "Do you mean that _____ ?" [fill in what you think is meant]; "Are you feeling _____ ?" [upset, angry, discouraged]; "Could you explain a little more about what you say happened?"; or even, "I don't understand what you just said."

- *Encourage further discussion.* If you feel the other person hasn't fully explained the situation or his or her point of view or feelings, encourage him or her to say a little more. A good way to do this is with open-ended comments, such as: "Could you say more about this?"; "Tell me more about it."; "How did you feel when . . .?"; or "Can you tell me why this is so important to you?" Be sure to express your question or comment in a neutral way to encourage the person to open up. Avoid a challenging tone, which implies that you are questioning the person's reasons for feeling or responding a certain way—an approach likely to put the person on the defensive. The idea is to pave the way for more discussion in both your question and your tone.

- *Use nonverbal listening responses to encourage the other person to continue talking.* Some examples of encouragement include smiling, leaning towards the speaker, nodding, and using eye contact. Also say things like "uhhuh" to show you are listening and are receptive.

Remember, your goal is to show that you hear and understand the other person, and care what he or she is saying. It might initially feel uncomfortable or insincere to repeatedly express what you are hearing and understanding. But with practice this approach will become natural. And if you take it seriously, you'll find that your increased concern for the other person and his or her satisfaction becomes genuine.

Expressing Your Own Feelings and Needs in a Nonthreatening Way

Besides using good communication skills to tone down the emotional level of a conflict, find out what the other person wants, and promote an open receptive climate to encourage conflict resolution, you can also use these skills to put forth your *own* feelings and needs. And you can do so in a way that reduces the chances for escalating or initiating a conflict.

A key way to do this is by using "I statements" or "I messages." This is a way of giving someone information about your own needs, feelings, or opinions in a nonthreatening, nonjudgmental way. You say what *you* want, think, or need, not what the other person needs to do or say. You are asserting yourself, but not putting pressure on the other person. That way the other person doesn't feel blamed, judged, or attacked; he or she won't feel cornered or respond defensively, thereby starting or upping the conflict.

"I statements" start with "I" and express a personal feeling or reaction. For example, if you need more time to respond to what the other person wants, you might say: "*I* would like some more time to think that over." Or if you have a difference of opinion with the other person, you might say: "*I* don't agree with you about that, and *I* would like to explain my own feelings about the matter." If you would like the other person to do something for you, you might comment in a neutral, requesting fashion: "I would appreciate it if you could do that for me as soon as possible."

By contrast, "you statements" or "you messages" can stir up conflicts because they can make it sound like you are blaming, judging, or attacking the other person, thus triggering a defensive response. Typical "you statements" include: "You're wrong," "You should do such and such," "You're inconsiderate," "You always do . . ."

One major problem with "you statements" is they sound like the person giving them believes she is right and the other person is wrong, when they really express the different opinion or point of view of the person making the statement. The way they are expressed, they can readily make the "you" feel angry and usually defensive. The person can feel accused or blamed, and thus feel a need to explain or defend him or herself. He or she may feel irate that the other person feels righteous or justified in making such a remark. The conflict then becomes not only about the original problem, but about the attitude of the person making the "you statements," which makes the original conflict even worse.

An example of this is when a parent is angry at a child for having done something wrong, such as leaving a messy room, and goes into accusatory mode. So instead of simply asking the child to clean up the room or offering some incentive so the child will keep the room clean in the future, the parent says something like: "You always leave the room a mess." Well, now the conflict is no longer just about the room. It's about what the child does and why, and about whether the child always does it, making child feel bad and resentful.

Similarly, couples often get into "you statement" behavior. They throw accusations at each other about something ("You never take out the garbage," "Why can't you be like So-and-so and do . . .") rather than focusing on the issue at hand ("Could we work out some arrangement about who takes out the garbage? Could you take it out on Monday, Wednesday and Friday?" or "I like it when you do . . .").

If you couch your "you statements" expressing what you want in a more neutral way, using the "I message" to soften them, you are more likely to create positive, productive communication. The other person is better able to listen and respond, without feeling confronted by a demand, blame, or threat.

Some examples of how you can turn these accusing "you statements" into more productive, communicative "I" statements are the following:

The basic model for using these "I messages" is to begin with a neutral, nonblameful description of the other's behavior that disturbs you. Explain your rational and emotional reactions to this behavior and why this behavior is a problem for you, or describe the effects on you of this behavior. Finally, state in gentle, assertive but not aggressive terms what you would like to see happen. Use words like "I would like," "I would appreciate," or "I would prefer."

The "I message" model, spelled out, looks something like this:

When you do _____ *(nonblameful description of the other's behavior), I feel* _____ *(your feelings or emotions about his behavior) because* _____ *(why his or her behavior is a problem for you or its effects on you), and I would like/appreciate/prefer* _____ *(what you want to happen).*

Summing Up: Communicating to Conquer Conflict

The way you communicate—and set the stage to help others communicate—can go a long way toward avoiding a conflict or dissipating one. The basic keys include the following:

*   Pay attention to nonverbal cues that suggest a discrepancy between what the speaker is thinking or feeling and what he or she is saying. Bring these issues out in the open.

*   Watch for hidden or wrong assumptions—your own or the other person's. Bring them out in the open so mistakes can be corrected.

*   Work towards open channels of communication. Say what you think or feel diplomatically, and encourage the other party to open up and talk to you, too.

*   Seek clarity. If something is unclear to you, ask for clarification so you understand. If someone else has trouble making themselves clear, see if you can figure out what he or she is saying and state

what you think he or she means, so you can provide the necessary explanations yourself. And of course, make sure your communications are clear to the listener.

- Learn to listen with interest, concern, and respect for the other person. Show empathy and show you hear and understand the speaker. Listen attentively without interruption or judgment. From time to time reflect back what you heard to show the other person you're following the conversation.

- Express your feelings and needs in a nonthreatening way, using "I statements." Avoid "you statements," which can make the other person feel judged, put down, or blamed.

Understanding the Different Conflict Styles

When you are in a conflict, one way to better deal with it is to recognize that you can choose among different styles of handling conflicts based on your personal style, the style of others involved in the conflict, and the nature of the conflict itself. I provided an overview of this approach in Chapter 3. Now I want to discuss these conflict styles in more detail, to both help you recognize these styles and learn when to best apply them in different situations.

Recognizing the Styles of Handling Conflict

There are five major styles of handling conflict. These have been described and used extensively in educational and business management programs based on a test called the Thomas-Kilmann Conflict Mode Instrument, developed by Kenneth W. Thomas and Ralph H. Kilmann in 1972. The word "Mode" in the title does double duty: it means, as on its face, "a method, manner, or style of acting or being," and at the same time is an acronym for "Management of Differences Exercise." When you take and score the test, you create a profile of your usual style or approach to dealing with conflict. The major conflict styles are derived from the common roots of all conflict: an incompatibility between the concerns of two or more parties.

Your style in dealing with a particular conflict depends on the degree to which you attempt to satisfy your own concern (by acting unassertively or assertively) and to satisfy the other party's concern (by acting cooperatively or uncooperatively).

When you put these two considerations together, they form a grid (previously introduced in Chapter 3), which is Thomas and Kilmann's method of identifying and labeling the five major styles of handling conflict.

The grid can be used to identify your style or anyone else's style. Begin by looking at the two rows of the grid labeled "unassertive" and "assertive." If your reaction is unassertive, you will tend to pull back from the conflict, whereas if your reaction is assertive, you'll be more aggressive and active in dealing with it. These are qualities you can recognize in others and recognize and control in yourself.

The columns of the grid deal with cooperation. If you are coopera-

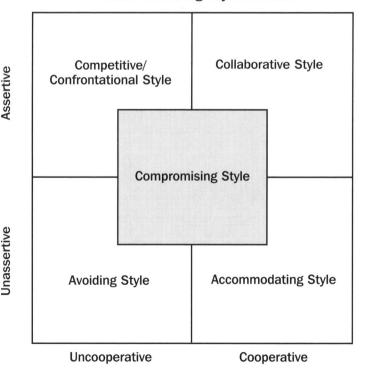

Conflict Handling Styles Matrix

| | Competitive/
Confrontational Style | Collaborative Style |

Compromising Style

Avoiding Style — Accommodating Style

Degree to Which You Attempt to Satisfy Your Own Concerns — Assertive / Unassertive

Uncooperative — Cooperative

Degree to Which You Attempt to Satisfy Others Co ncerns

tive, you'll try to work with the person or the group you are having a conflict with; if you are uncooperative, you'll seek to resolve the issue in your own way or not deal with it at all. The degree of cooperation offered should also be readily identifiable in yourself and others.

When you put these rows and columns together, you get a matrix of the five styles with the compromising style in the middle. This compromising approach represents a balance of being cooperative and uncooperative, unassertive and assertive.

As you look more closely at these different styles, you may recognize one or another as the more usual ways you tend to deal with a conflict yourself, and that other people you know tend to use certain styles more often. You'll also find that under certain conditions you may be more likely to use one style rather than another, and others will similarly be more drawn to a different approach under those same conditions. While everyone may try all the styles at some point, people have certain style preferences. Certain styles might also be more appropriate and more effective in resolving particular types of conflict, and these may or may not match the usual styles you or others use. So there can be some complexity in assessing your own and other's styles and matching these to what works best in dealing with a particular conflict.

I've described each style below. These were touched on in Chapter 3, but are explained in more detail here. Then I will discuss the ways of applying each style at the end of the chapter.

The Competitive Style

As the grid shows, a person who uses a competitive style is very assertive and interested in getting his or her own way. He or she isn't particularly interested in cooperating with others, but instead approaches a conflict in a very forceful, confrontational way, less concerned with others think than in getting his or her own way. Or as Thomas and Kilmann describe the dynamic, you strive primarily to satisfy your concern at the expense of others by forcing people to do it your way, arguing, or pulling rank. You use your power to win your objective, and if you have enough power, you can often do that.

This can be a good style to use if you are in a position of power; you know your idea or approach is right for the situation, and you are able to prevail over others. However, it's probably not the kind of approach to use in personal relationships where you want to get along with people; the competitive/confrontational style frequently alienates people. It's also not a very effective style to use when you don't have a lot of power in a situation, such as in a disagreement with your boss. If you come on too forcefully, you might get yourself fired.

More specifically, some of the times when this is a good style to use are when:

- You have authority to make the decision, and it seems clear that this is the one best way.
- A decision has to be made quickly, and you have the power to make it.
- You feel you have no other options and you have nothing to lose.
- You are in an emergency situation where immediate decisive action is necessary.
- You can't get a group to agree, you feel you are at an impasse, and someone must make the group move ahead.
- You have to make an unpopular decision, but action is required now, and you have the power to make that choice.

You may not be particularly popular when you use this approach, although you may win admirers if your solution works. But this isn't the style to use if being popular and well-liked is your primary objective. Rather, use it to get your way in something that is important to you, when you feel you must act quickly to get your way immediately, and when you feel confident you will win because you have the power or position to do so.

The Avoiding Style

The second major approach is when you don't assert yourself, don't cooperate, avoid the conflict entirely, or delay dealing with it. This might be a good approach when the problem situation is not that important to you, when you don't want to be hassled about it, or when you feel you are in a no-win situation. You might also use avoidance when you feel you are wrong and the other person is right, or when the other person has more power—all good reasons to decide it's not worth standing up for your position in a conflict. Some ways to do this include changing the subject, walking out of the room, or acting to put the conflict aside or delay it, so you don't have to deal with the matter now or at all. In short, you don't attempt to satisfy either your or the other person's concern. Instead, you sidestep the conflict by ignoring it, passing the buck, delaying, or otherwise avoiding the issue.

Avoidance can be a good approach to use if you're faced with dealing with a difficult person and there is no strong reason to be or work together. The approach can also be useful if you are unsure about making a decision and don't have to decide immediately. Instead of getting tense about trying to resolve the situation right away, you might give yourself the luxury of extra time and avoid deciding for the present. Remember, however, that you will likely to have to face the issue eventually, so while a temporary avoidance may work for a time, irresponsibly turning away from an issue may not.

Another good time to use the avoiding style is when you feel you don't have enough information to resolve a particular situation. If you can wait and time might provide the answer, it may be best to acknowledge that a delay is advantageous and explain: "I can't deal with this now. Let's wait."

Below are more specific situations where you might want to use the avoiding style.

- Tensions are too high, and you feel a need to cool down.
- The issue isn't very important to you or you feel it's objectively a trivial issue that's not worth dealing with.
- You're having a bad day, and there's a good chance you might not deal with the issue properly.
- You know you can't, or probably won't, win in the conflict.
- You want to buy more time, perhaps because you need to get more information or get some assistance from others.
- The situation is complex and difficult to change, so you feel tackling it will just be a wasted effort.
- You have little power to resolve the situation or to get it resolved in a desirable way.
- You feel that others have a better chance of resolving the situation.
- There's danger in trying to deal with the situation at the moment, since bringing the conflict out into the open might make the situation worse.

Though some people may consider avoidance as "running away" from the issue rather than using than a valid conflict management technique, evasion or delay can occasionally be an appropriate and constructive response to a problem. Perhaps if you ignore it, say nothing, leave, drop the subject, or shift your and others' attention to something else, the conflict will resolve itself. If not, you can deal with it later when you and others feel more up to it. However, be careful in using this approach, since others may believe you are just procrastinating or being irresponsible. So use it judiciously, when it seems most appropriate and wise to do so.

The Accommodating Style

The third style is the accommodating approach. This occurs when you work cooperatively with the other person, without trying to assert your own concerns. You give in or defer to what the other person wants. You might take this approach when the outcome of the situation is very important to the other person but less so to you. Also, you might be accommodating when you feel you can't win because the other person has more power; you just give in and go along with what the other person wants. Thomas and Kilmann describe this style by saying that when you accommodate, you sacrifice your own concern in order to satisfy another's concern by conceding, taking pity on that person, or otherwise acceding to what they want.

Since you put your own concerns aside in using this approach, it's most appropriate to do this when you don't have a lot invested in a situation, or a lot at stake in the outcome. And, of course, this is a perfectly appropriate style when you have no choice and it's either like it or endure it anyway, as when a boss gives a firm order. When you don't have a big investment or stake in the matter, accommodating lets you feel comfortable, and you won't resent going along with what the other person wants.

If you feel you will be giving up something important to you and don't feel good about that (unless this is an "accept or else" situation), then the accommodating style is probably not appropriate. The same might be true if you feel the other person hasn't given up enough in return or doesn't appreciate what you have given. It's the type of approach to use when you feel you are not losing too much by giving something up. Or try using this strategy to smooth things over for the time being, and plan to raise the subject again. Later on, you can seek an outcome more in line with your desired position.

Accommodation can be a little bit like avoidance, since you can use it to delay finding a true resolution to a problem. But the difference is that in accommodation you cooperate; you address the situation and agree to do what the other person wants. When you use avoidance, you don't do anything to further the other person's desires and just push the situation away.

Some of the best times to consider accommodating are:

- When you don't really care that much what happens
- When you want to keep the peace and maintain harmony with others
- When you feel it is more important to maintain a relationship with someone than get the matter decided your way
- When you recognize that the outcome is much more important to the other person than to you
- When you recognize that you are wrong and the other person is right
- When you have little power or little chance of winning
- When you think the other person might learn from the situation if you go along with what he wants, even though you don't agree with what he is doing or think he is making a mistake

By giving in, agreeing, or sacrificing your own concerns to what the other person wants, you may be able to smooth over a bad situation and restore harmony. You might then continue to go along with this outcome, if it feels all right to you. Or you might use this period of smoothing things over to work on finding a final resolution you would prefer.

The Collaborative Style

The fourth style is the collaborative approach. In this approach, you get actively involved in working out a conflict by asserting what you want, while still trying to cooperate with the other person. This style can take a little longer to work through than the other ways of handling conflict, since you first want to get all of the issues and concerns you both have on the table, and then listen to each other's needs. But if you have the time and the issue is important enough, this is a good way to find a win-win situation that satisfies the needs of all parties.

This style works particularly well when the parties have different underlying needs. In such cases, the source of dissatisfaction may be hard to pin down. It may appear initially that you both want the same thing (and only one can have it), or that you have opposing goals, both of which are the immediate sources of conflict. However, often there is a difference between the surface issues or positions in dispute and the underlying interests or needs, which are the real sources of conflict.

For example, the surface issue creating a conflict at work may be an employee's lateness. But that lateness may only mask a deeper conflict: that the man is dissatisfied with his work—he feels a lack of respect, acknowledgment, or responsibility, and he is responding by exhibiting a growing disconnection from his work. If only the surface issue is dealt with, this will result in a superficial treatment that is likely not to have long-term effectiveness, because the roots of the problem remain. The man might stop being late. But then he might engage in some unconscious or not-so-unconscious acts of sabotage at work, take some extra break time, or help himself to office facilities or supplies, telling himself he deserves them because he is underpaid and underappreciated. That would be his way of making up some extra compensation to himself.

By contrast, using a collaborative approach encourages each person to bring all of his true needs and desires into the open, so they can be addressed. The man in the above situation might point out that he feels a need for more recognition, appreciation, and responsibility. If the boss understands this, he might be willing to offer more, leading the man to become more committed to his work again, thereby ending the lateness problem as well as having other positive effects.

Thus, the key to a successful collaboration involves taking the time to look at underlying interests and needs in the hopes of finding a way to meet the real needs of both parties. By working together, you can search for new alternatives or work out good compromises once you both understand all the issues.

More specifically, this approach can work well under the following conditions:

- When the issues are very important to both or all parties, and no one is willing to let go entirely
- When you have a close, continuing, or interdependent relationship with the other party
- When you have the time to deal with the problem, such as on a long-term project

- When both you and the other party are aware of the problem and are clear about what you want

- When both you and the other party are willing to put some thought and work into finding a solution

- When you both have the skills to articulate your concerns and to listen to what others have to say

- When you and others in the conflict have a similar amount of power, or are willing to put aside any power differences to work together as equals in coming up with a solution

While collaboration is thus an amicable, thoughtful approach towards getting everyone's needs recognized and met, it takes a certain amount of work and effort. All parties have to make a commitment in time, and they have to be able to clarify their wants, express their needs, listen to others do the same, explore alternatives, and agree to solutions. Without any one of these elements, this approach won't work. Collaboration is thus more complicated than other approaches, but it can result in the most mutually satisfying resolution to a serious and important conflict.

The Compromising Style

In the center of the matrix is the compromise approach. You give up a little bit of what you want to get the rest of what you want, and the other parties in the conflict do the same. Or in Thomas-Kilmann terms, you settle for a partial satisfaction of your concern and a partial satis- faction of the other's concern. You do this by making exchanges and concessions, and by bargaining to come up with a compromise solution you each can agree on.

To some extent, such acts may sound like collaboration. But com- promise occurs on a more superficial level. You give up something, the other person gives up something, and you come to a resolution. You are not searching for underlying needs and interests as in collaboration. You are dealing only with what people say they want.

A compromise approach might be especially appropriate when you and another person want the same thing, and you both can't end up getting it. For instance, you both want the same office, or you want to spend the same vacation time doing something different. So you work out a compromise based on giving up a little bit of what you each want to do, which can be an especially appropriate approach in an office that believes in empowering workers or creating employee-led teams (where employees get to make many of their own decision about their work arrangements). In the office case, for example, you might work out something like: "You take the office for four hours in the morning and I'll take the office for four hours in the afternoon." In the vacation case, your compromise might be something like: "We'll go to the mountains for part of the vacation, if you're willing to spend the other part on the beach."

By contrast, in the collaborative approach your focus is on resolving underlying issues and needs, so you would search for the underlying needs and attempt to work out an arrangement based on that. For instance, in discussing the office, you might come to realize that your need really isn't for that particular office; you really just want the recognition that goes with it and can get that recognition in other, more important ways. In a compromise, you deal with the conflict situation as given and look for ways to influence or alter those givens through giving in on different positions or making exchanges.

Another difference is that the goal of collaboration is a long-term win-win solution; in compromise, the outcome may be more short-term and expedient. So after a successful compromise, a person might agree: "I can live with that," since the emphasis is not on win-win, but on "We can't both get what we want, so let's work out something we can each live with."

In such situations, collaboration may not even be possible. Perhaps neither of you has the time or the energy to devote to it, or you have mutually exclusive goals. A compromise would be the best way to go.

More specifically, the times when a compromise is most appropriate include the following:

- When you have the same amount of power as someone else and you are both committed to mutually exclusive goals.
- When you want to achieve a resolution quickly, because of time pressures or because it's more economical and efficient that way.
- When you can settle for a temporary resolution.
- When you will benefit from a short-term gain.
- When you haven't been able to work out a solution through collaboration or a more competitive/forceful approach, and compromise alone offers *some* solution.

- When the goals are not extremely important to you, and you are willing to modify your objectives.

- When a compromise will make a relationship or agreement work, and you'd rather have that than nothing at all.

Compromise is often a good fallback or last resort for achieving a resolution. You might even choose it initially when you don't have the power to get what you want, can't work out a collaboration, and don't want to give in or avoid the issue. By compromising, you at least can get part of your agenda while the other party gets part of his—and you can always try another conflict resolution approach later if your initial compromise doesn't provide the long-term answer.

When you do seek a compromise with someone, start by clarifying your respective wants and needs. Then look for areas of agreement. Make suggestions and listen to what the other person suggests, and be ready to make offers, exchanges, and bargains. Negotiate until you can find a mutually agreeable formula on what each of you will give up and get in return. Ideally, you'll both be satisfied with the compromise.

Recognizing Your Own Approach to Conflict

All of these conflict styles are appropriate at different times, and no one style is better than another. Optimally, you should be able to use any of these styles effectively and consciously choose when it is best to use each one. The best approach depends on the particular factors in each situation and on what feels most comfortable to you. While it's natural to prefer certain styles, strict style preferences may limit you: You may avoid or mishandle the most appropriate style for a particular conflict. Thus, be aware of both your own style preferences and the range of alternatives. This puts you in a better position to make choices in handling conflict situations.

If you notice that you are likely to avoid using a particular style or don't feel comfortable or competent using it, try working on your ability to use that style. For example, if you tend to accommodate others too much rather than sticking up for your own position, work on being more assertive and forceful, so you can use the competitive style when the situation warrants. Or if you compromise too much because you are impatient to get to a solution, learn to slow down in handling important issues. Sometimes patient collaboration will help you find a better solution.

To develop your repertoire for resolving conflicts, first assess your usual style of approaching conflict. Chances are that you tend to use one or two modes most commonly, just as a performer has a characteristic style or repertoire of performance. In some cases, you may have one style that is especially predominant—your primary approach—and other styles you commonly use but less often: your secondary or tertiary styles. If you have two equally characteristic styles, such as accommodation and avoidance, since you'll do anything to prevent a conflict, then you are considered "bimodal." Should you have three characteristic styles—such as fight, flight, or compromise—you are "trimodal."

Thomas and Kilmann developed a test they call the Conflict Mode Instrument, designed to give each person a profile of scores showing how he responds to conflict. They developed the test by questioning groups of managers and using their answers as a baseline against which to measure everyone else. When you take the test, your responses are scored relative to the managers in each conflict style or modality.

Taking this test can be very helpful in giving you some insight into yourself, though you can also do a self-assessment by reviewing your usual and preferred responses in previous conflicts you have experienced. Commonly, you will already have a sense of your preferred styles, though the test will help you look at your approach objectively by examining your reactions to a wide range of situations.

When I took the test myself with a group of managers in the nonprofit sector, most of us were fairly accurate in assessing our habitual ways of dealing with conflict, though the test provided confirmation. For example, when I first took the test, I found I was relatively high in competing, avoiding, and compromising, but fairly low in collaborating and accommodating. I had sensed in advance that this would be likely, since I like to reach a decision quickly, focus on getting what I want, but don't feel most issues are important enough to fight for my own way—more or less the choose-your-battles approach. Still, the test helped me realize how I could gain by learning to collaborate and introducing my needs into negotiation. Likewise, others who took the test with me sensed how they might score in advance and found the test helped them to further understand the patterns they recognized in their everyday lives.

Should you change over time, the test will reflect this, and you will probably recognize these changes yourself. For example, when I took the test again later, feeling more aggressive and assertive, I was indeed even higher in competition and compromise. The test reflected my own changes over time.

By the same token, you can take the test yourself or give yourself a quick overall assessment by thinking about the five styles, and asking yourself some questions about how and when you use each one. Then, you can rate yourself on which you think you use most, use best, use least, and feel most comfortable using. The first chart, How I Usually Respond to Conflict Situations (page 127), will help you organize your responses. As you go through this process, write down the first response that comes into mind; this is usually the most accurate, because it is the most spontaneous and the most intuitive. Also, in responding, don't try to think of how you responded to the latest conflict situation you were in or the most dramatic. Rather, review the way you have responded to conflict situations *generally* over the years. And don't try to think of the way you would like to respond—there is no right or wrong way to respond; it all depends on the situation.

You can always expand your repertoire of conflict responses in the future, based on developing your ability to use other conflict styles. But for now, just give your initial reaction to how you usually respond when faced with a conflict. The chart should give you an overall picture of how you are most and least likely to respond, and how you feel about using these different methods.

Rank what you consider your usual style of responding to conflict from 1 (high) to 5 (low) in each column based on how much you think you use that style in dealing with most conflict situations you encounter. If you feel unsure about a ranking, consider the ranking a tie. Then, skip to the next number for the following rank. (That is, if two styles tie for first place in a category, give the third style the number 3 for third.)

Assessing Your Approach to Conflict

Once you have a clearer picture of how you generally deal with conflict, you can consider how you feel about using your primary approach and whether you might benefit from developing your ability to use other styles. To do this, review the conflicts you have been in and consider what styles you have used. In some situations, you may have used several different approaches.

How I Usually Respond to Conflict Situations

Method of Use and Attitude Toward Using

Conflict Style	Use the Most	Like Using the Most	Use the Least	Feel the Least Comfortable Using
Competitive/Confrontational (I actively seek to get my own way)				
Avoiding (I seek to avoid the conflict situation)				
Accommodating (I seek to work out a mutually satisfying solution with others)				
Collaborative (I seek to work out a mutually satisfying solution with others)				
Compromising (I seek to work out a solution in which we each give up a little to get some of what we want)				

Then, look at the outcome for each of these situations. Was your approach to the conflict effective? Did you get what you wanted? Did the other party? Do you feel the approach you used helped achieve a favorable result? Or do you feel your approach didn't work? If so, what approach might you have used with a better result?

Here are some examples of how you might use this process.

- If you tend to be a highly *competitive* person in your approach to conflict, you usually push to get your own way and like to see things happen quickly. At times when you are in a power position and can push things through, this confrontational approach may work. You may get other people to agree with you and do what you want. But sometimes, even though you get outward agreement, this approach may result in negative spin-offs. People may resent you and try to get back at you in other ways, such as through gossip or sabotage. You might also notice other times when this approach hasn't worked from the outset. Perhaps it has led other competitive people to resist and fight for what they want as well.

• If you tend to *avoid* issues, look at how well that approach has worked for you. Do you feel comfortable at putting many conflicts out of sight? Or do you regret not having achieved a solution?

• If you tend to *accommodate,* ask whether giving in has generally worked well for you. Do you feel okay about supporting what the other person wants to do? Or do you feel any anger or resentment when your needs remain unmet?

• If you tend to *compromise,* you might ask yourself if your interest in expedience is getting in your way of finding a better, more enduring solution.

• If you are primarily a *collaborator,* consider if you might be spending more time than necessary in resolving your conflicts.

Through this exercise, you remind yourself that there are numerous ways to approach any conflict, all of which can be useful. You may already be using all of them, though you may not be consciously planning where, when, or how best to use them. Your more usual approaches may be fine in many cases. But in other cases, it may be better to use a different approach. Reviewing past conflict experiences can help you see how well your current styles are working for you (and for others you encounter). You may find you need to be more open to using other approaches. If so, you can work on developing your ability to use them now, so you can consciously draw on any approach for managing conflicts in the future.

The exercise on the next page will help you pinpoint particular areas of weakness where you need to further develop your ability to use a style. Also, it will help you be more aware of the way you make choices and respond in a conflict, so you can deal better with conflicts in the future. By being aware, you can actively *choose* the response you want to make. Also, you will develop a sense of objectivity, so you can stand back from yourself in a conflict situation and choose rationally what you want to do.

Use the second chart, Assessing the Effectiveness of My Use of

Conflict Handling Styles (page 130), to list some of the major conflicts you have experienced. For each one, note the conflict style or styles you used; rate each style's overall effectiveness; and note the result of using that style, whether favorable or unfavorable. Finally, note what other approach (or approaches) you might have used with a better result. For each alternate approach you list, picture going through with that style. Ask yourself: What would I have said? What are the likely reactions of others and myself? How would that relationship work differently now if you used that approach?

Assessing the Effectiveness of My Use of Conflict Handling Styles

Conflict Situation	Style Used	Overall Effectiveness (–3 to +3)	Result of Using That Style (describe benefits or negative outcomes)	Alternate Approach	Why Better

10

Choosing the Best
Conflict Style

The conflict handling styles described in the last chapter provide a framework for looking at how you deal with conflict and choosing the most appropriate style. This chapter looks more closely at how to better choose and *use* these styles.

Assessing the Balance of Power

Two key considerations in choosing an effective conflict style are the following:

1. The other person's position of power, relative to yours (how much power he or she has)

2. The other person's perspective (where he or she is coming from)

If you have more power than the other person, you may be able to use a competitive style, so you come on forcefully to get what you want. You can get the other person to give in (that is, to accommodate you). But if the other person has more power than you and comes on strong, you may need to be the one to accommodate.

If you try to compromise when power is unequal, the power differential plays a key role in the conflict's outcome. Unless the more powerful person agrees to put position considerations aside, whoever has more power usually ends up with a better deal in a compromise. That person has the bargaining chips to get more of what he or she wants.

Of course, the particular situation will also affect your response even when someone else has a lot of power. If you are dealing with a high-powered person who is coming on strong, it may not work well to come on strong yourself: You will probably just end up butting heads, and if the person is more powerful than you, you may well lose. So think about how much you want to achieve your goal, and whether or not you can win in a power struggle that stands in your way. If you feel what you want is important enough, perhaps you can pull together the support of others to counteract that person's high level of power or even tough it out on your own. But if you feel you are in a no-win situation or have a great risk of losing in an out-and-out conflict, you may need to accommodate the other person and pull back. This is especially true if your potential loss is high: your job, a friend, or a co-worker's respect.

Even if there is no power differential, but the other person feels very strongly about something, you may have good reasons to pull back. Say a good friend has certain ideas you disagree with; it may be better to go along with him at times, rather than challenging him. You can avert a major blowup and demonstrate the high value you place on your relationship with that friend.

Power differentials also affect your ability to collaborate with someone. While the other person's perspective can be very important when you are trying to collaborate or work out a fair compromise, to do either successfully you have to be on a relatively equal level of power or be willing to put power considerations aside. But being equal or putting aside differences in power isn't enough. You also need to be dealing with someone who is willing to discuss things with you honestly and sincerely. If not, the other person may try to take advantage of you as you show signs of giving in. Then, you may find that your attempts to collaborate or compromise are pushed aside by the other person's more forceful competitive spirit, seeking to pressure you into giving in and making concessions—in short, making you into an accommodator. Thus, for any collaboration or compromise to work well, you both need to proceed in good faith. If you feel the other person does not share your commitment to collaborate or compromise, it may be better not to use that particular style, since you will end up being forced to give in.

The ideal is to aim for a fair, good-faith approach in settling a conflict. But you must learn to recognize those situations where power or perspective differences leave you vulnerable to a competitive or exploitive person. In such cases, it's best to acknowledge the differences early on and choose a more self-protective approach.

Recognizing Your Priorities

While it's important to keep your needs in mind in seeking to resolve a conflict, don't let them blind you and block you from achieving a resolution. You must allow room for the other person's needs as well.

Also, put your needs in perspective in order to recognize your priorities. You need to consider the importance of your goal relative to the opposition you must overcome to achieve it. If your goal is worth it, it may be appropriate to take a more forceful stand to achieve it in a particular situation. Or you might find a way to attain that goal by pulling out of the situation to avoid the conflict. Alternatively, you may have other priorities, such as keeping the peace in a relationship or keeping a job, which suggest backing down or compromising as better, more practical approaches—at least for now.

That's what happened for Gary, who complained at a workshop about feeling trapped in a situation he hated at work. He worked as a computer programmer and was a quiet, introverted person who found the aggressive office politicking and jostling for power depressing. He was especially perturbed that his manager was constantly putting him down and telling him what to do and when. She seemed to ignore what he said whenever he tried to speak up.

Gary wasn't sure what to do. Should he be assertive and use a more competitive, confrontational approach to stand up to her? Give in and accommodate? Avoid the situation entirely by finding another job? Or was some sort of compromise or collaboration possible? Since his boss had so much more power, he doubted that he had any option but to give in, as he was doing. But that left him feeling resentful.

To decide what to do, Gary had to first look at his priorities and consider the probable outcomes of using different conflict response styles. Accordingly, in the workshop, I asked him to list and rate his priorities. What was most important? Keeping his job? Finding a new one? Standing up to his manager to get his way, no matter the cost?

Gary began examining the possible options and likely outcomes. After considering the competitive approach first, Gary realized it wasn't worth it to combat his boss directly, because she had more power and liked to get her own way, so a competitive approach probably wouldn't work. Since she had more power, she would win and he might even lose his job.

As for the accommodation approach he was already using, it was keeping his boss happy and his job secure, though Gary was miserable. But at least he could work on changing his attitude so he wouldn't be miserable, such as by using personal avoidance techniques along with accommodation. That way, he could insulate himself psychologically from the personal fallout caused by yielding to what his boss wanted him to do.

The avoidance techniques that Gary eventually decided to use are ones you too can use to protect yourself from negative feelings you have about giving in:

- Do some visualizations or internal exercises, telling yourself: "I'm not going to let this bother me."
- Put up a protective shield or wall of white energy around yourself by visualizing it or telling yourself it is there. Then, use this wall of energy to deflect any negative feelings bouncing off this shield or wall, while you stay centered and safe from attack.
- Remind yourself that if you are going to continue to work in the same place, you have to deal with a person you don't like. Just keep telling yourself that it's one of the conditions that goes with the job and you can't let working with that person get to you.

If Gary had felt the situation was *too* oppressive, this accommodation-avoidance approach would not work very well. In this case, it might be better for Gary to avoid the situation entirely by quitting or transferring to a new department, if possible. So if things do get too bad, remember that leaving is always an option, and a perfectly honorable and mentally healthy way to go.

Finally, Gary considered the collaboration and compromise options. Neither seemed a likely possibility, because his boss had so much more power than he did and both of these approaches require relatively equal footing—so each party can give some and take some—and they rarely work in unequal power situations. So don't try to collaborate or compromise if you face a nonreceptive powerful adversary.

In sum, given Gary's low power position, his only real choices were accommodation and avoidance if he wanted to keep his job, or leaving if accommodation and avoidance were too painful for him. Since he wanted to stay, he decided to make accommodation more comfortable for him by counteracting his feelings of resentment with internal avoidance techniques, at least until he could arrange a transfer to another department with a new supervisor. Likewise, in any difficult situation, if you have to give in even though you don't want to, you might combine accommodation with an internal avoidance technique. When you detach yourself emotionally from the situation, you might feel better about any concessions you have to make.

Becoming Aware of Real Issues and Interests

Besides looking beneath your surface desires to consider your priorities, look beneath them to assess your own and the other party's deeper needs and interests. Your surface wants, demands, or positions are what may spark the conflict, because your wants, demands, or positions seem to be incompatible with the other person's. However, these may be symptoms of the deeper concerns that are of greatest importance to each of you. While it may not be possible to satisfy the seemingly important surface desires, you may find ways to resolve those important underlying needs or concerns.

Becoming aware of what you really need and really want is thus a key to achieving these goals and working towards a solution to the conflict. This awareness will help you recognize those situations when it's not worth struggling towards a resolution. The three types of awareness to have are:

1. Awareness of your own surface wants and underlying interests

2. Awareness of the other party's surface wants and underlying interests

3. Awareness of what you and the other person require to satisfy these wants or needs

The two ways to develop this awareness are:

1. Get the issues and interests out in the open and talk about them directly.

2. Use your sensitivity or intuition to look underneath the surface. Learn what is really going on for the person with whom you are in conflict.

While it may be necessary to get to underlying interests to forge a long-term, satisfying resolution when these deeper interests are very important, in many everyday situations you may not want to take the time to deal with these. It's more efficient to find an alternative way to deal with the conflict.

For example, if the conflict is over your neighbor parking in front of your house on a public street when it is more convenient for you to park your extra car there, it may not be worth the time it takes to discuss the underlying issues (your convenience and your feeling of security in being able to see your car from your window versus your neighbor's convenience and the right to park freely on the public streets). Rather, it might be more expedient to simply work out a compromise, such as not doing something he doesn't like in return for his finding an alternate parking space (for example, you won't honk your horn to hurry up your kids for school in the morning).

Alternatively, recognize those situations where you need to dig deeper and choose an appropriate style, such as if a friend seems very unhappy about what seems to you a trivial matter, like turning down an invitation to a social occasion. Consider that he or she might have deep-rooted, concealed interests, such as issues around rejection and not feeling good enough. Such an awareness might lead you to accommodate that person (say by dropping in to say hello for a half-hour before you go on to do something else) and consider your surface wants (going to another event) less important than that person's deeper needs.

In some cases, this awareness might lead you to seek to collaborate if your needs seem equally important. For example, if you discuss your plans to go to another party that night but mention you would be glad to drop in, it may turn out that what your friend would really prefer to do is cancel his or her own party and join you in going to this larger, more happening event. By having this discussion, you find out what you each really wants to do, and the resolution may be a real win for your both.

To have such a discussion, encourage the other person to share his or her needs using a technique such as active listening. Also, it helps to get your own underlying needs and interests out in the open during a collaboration, and here's where visualization and self-awareness techniques can help.

In sum, recognize that different types of wants and needs can exist;

you can then choose which level to deal with and which approaches can best help you address particular wants and needs in order to resolve a conflict.

Being Aware of Your Options for Response

Though it may take some time to know when to apply the different strategies, as you keep thinking about and using them this awareness will become a natural part of your life. You will be better able to respond appropriately when you encounter any conflict or potential conflict. In fact, after a while, you will become so aware that your awareness will become unconscious or automatic, as if you were on autopilot.

For example, suppose you are in an ongoing conflict with a neighbor or co-worker whenever you encounter each other. Initially, you might approach the conflict consciously thinking about what conflict handling approach to use. Perhaps you might sort through the different styles, thinking something like: "Well, this particular approach didn't work before, so what other approach might I try now?"

This strategy of *consciously* thinking about your own situation in light of the description of each separate style is a good way to begin. But from experience, soon you'll be able to choose easily what style is most appropriate and most comfortable in each situation, whether it is standing up for your rights, walking away, or otherwise accommodating, compromising, or trying to find a resolution through collaboration. You'll create your own expertise and catalogue of effective and not-so-effective approaches.

Using a Series of Strategies to Deal with a Conflict

One appropriate style may be all you need to resolve some conflicts. But in other cases, you may need to use a combination of styles, particularly if you are dealing with a complex or ongoing conflict. Or you may find one style useful to resolve a part of the conflict, but require a different style to deal with other parts of it. And one style may resolve the conflict for a time, but if the conflict resurfaces, you may need to use another style to more completely resolve it.

For example, suppose a conflict with co-workers erupts when you are under a great deal of pressure, so you don't want to spend much time resolving the problem right now. You might start off by using avoidance to delay dealing with the issue. But then one of your co-workers comes to you asking for some immediate help to respond to a deadline, making you feel even more resentful because of the unresolved disagreement you already have. Yet, because of the deadline, you might feel it appropriate to accommodate the person temporarily. Then, once the time pressure is over, you can sit down, air your concerns, and work towards some mutually agreeable solution through compromise or collaboration.

As you pay more attention to working through conflicts, you will become more sensitive to the appropriate approach to use. It helps to stay flexible, so you can shift strategies if your first attempt at resolution isn't working.

Also, in some situations you might use any number of styles to deal with different aspects of the conflict. For instance, in an involved negotiation over a long-term business deal or a personal relationship, you might: 1) compromise to get some initial points of disagreement out of the way, 2) accommodate to the other person's greater needs in another area, 3) press competitively for what you really want on some issue, 4) avoid dealing with other topics you consider less important, and 5) use collaboration for the most deeply felt concerns both you and the other person have.

The best way to sharpen your skills in using and choosing among the styles is real-life practice. The exercises below can help to prepare you for these real-life conflicts by enabling you to preplan what you might do, so you will feel more confident and assured when the time comes.

Exercise #1: Visualization

By playing out a conflict or even a brief encounter in your mind in advance, you can anticipate the results of different approaches. This will help you pick out the style most likely to succeed while you still have a chance to use it. This anticipatory visualization may also give you the needed distance and objectivity to gain insights into the motivations and fears of different parties in the conflict.

The following visualization exercise will help you try out different approaches. Read the script below into a tape recorder or keep the guidelines in mind to create your own visualization. If you record it, read through the script and make any changes to tailor it to your situation. Once you've recorded it in a soothing, authoritative voice, find a quiet place to listen, close your eyes, and concentrate.

Start off by getting relaxed. Focus on your breathing. Feel your chest and stomach expand with each breath, and release. Just close your eyes and pay attention, as you let your breathing go in, and out; in, and out; in, and out. As you get relaxed, you will stay alert and awake, and pay attention to the sound of my voice.

Now, imagine a screen in a theater. You're in the theater looking at the screen, and some problem situation comes to mind. You might see yourself on the screen, and maybe you see other people, too.

It might be a situation at work. It might be a situation involving a friend or family member. It might be an internal situation. It could be something you have to make a decision about now. Or maybe it's something you could put off for a week, two weeks, or more. It might be a conflict situation that just happened, or it might be an ongoing situation.

Whatever the conflict situation is, you see it on the screen and watch it play itself out. You feel a certain distance from it, because you're sitting in the audience watching. And even though you may be a character in the scene, you're also removed from it, because you are just observing it, too.

Now, as you watch, imagine the different approaches you might use to resolve the conflict.

First, maybe you want to achieve an important objective, so try taking an assertive style, a more competitive style, to do what you want to get the situation resolved in your way. If you do, notice what you say; notice how others react. And notice how others feel.

Or perhaps you are seeing something that's not that important to you. You're willing to give in and let go of it. If so, you might want to adopt a more accommodative style. If you do, notice what that feels like.

Or maybe this is the kind of conflict you want to avoid. You'd like to put it away or walk away from it, if you can. In this case, you might choose the avoidance style and leave. If so, think about what would happen if you walked away.

Or, if you can't leave physically, visualize yourself with a protective screen of white light around you. This protective screen keeps the conflict away from you, so you don't have to think about it or pay attention to it. Yet, at any time you can drop this protection to deal with the conflict in another way. So notice how this approach feels to you and how it works.

Or, if this conflict is important and worth resolving carefully, you need to take the time and effort to work things out. If so, perhaps there is one person you need to talk to in order, to work out this resolution. Now, if you want, picture yourself talking to this person, working together, collaborating to achieve a resolution.

Or if you are experiencing a conflict going back and forth in your own mind, you may want to take the time to deal with this and work out a resolu-

tion. So now imagine two parts of yourself sitting down and talking about the conflict, one side with one point of view, and the other with an opposing view. As they talk, each side expresses its needs and attempts to find common interests.

Finally, maybe this is a situation where you can give a little and the other person can give a little towards a compromise. Or if it's an internal conflict, part of you can give a little and another part of you can give a little. So maybe a compromise might work. If so, picture what this compromise might look like.

Now, having reviewed the possible conflict styles you can choose, recall which felt the most right, for you can choose among any of those styles. Choose now and see it play on the screen.

Now watch yourself making a decision and choosing a particular style. Or imagine yourself choosing a series of styles to deal with the problem now. Or if you don't want to look at the problem at this time, you can always use avoidance for now, and deal with the problem later.

If any questions or problems come up in using any particular style, they will come to mind now. You may have other questions you must resolve first in order to resolve your conflict. Let any of these questions or problems come to mind now, and notice what you need to do to resolve them.

Now, whatever style you have chosen, you see the problem resolved. You see your ideal solution occurring before you. You see your goal, and you experience a feeling of peace and harmony.

So now you're feeling very good and very comfortable with that solution. And you know you can always use that approach again when other conflicts come up. You can always go to the theater and see the conflict on the screen in front of you. You can always choose among these different styles. You can watch each possibility played out, and then see the conflict resolved.

Now, feeling very good on seeing this resolution, let the issue go. See the conflict on the screen or the resolution you have achieved slowly dissipate. Watch it fade away.

Now notice the credit on the screen. You can thank yourself, because your name is up there as the director. You are totally in charge of this conflict and in resolving it. And you're up there, too, as the scriptwriter. And you're there as the starring actor.

You feel very, very good about having this control. And you feel very good about the creativity you've shown in resolving the conflict.

Now the credits are finished. You start getting up from the movie theater, and as you walk out into the light, I'll start counting backwards from five to one. As I do, you'll become more and more awake and come back into the room. Five, four, more and more awake. Three, back into the room. Two. One. And when you are ready, open your eyes and come back in the room.

Exercise #2: Mapping Out Possibilities

Sometimes it helps to write down or map out the possible approaches to a conflict using a more analytical, logical approach to conflict resolution instead of using a visualization. To do this, begin by clarifying the problem. Ask yourself if this is a one-time conflict or part of a recurring pattern. The latter requires a more general and comprehensive response.

Once the issue is clearer in your mind, you can look at how you might apply each approach you are considering to the problem. This includes considering the various ways the other party might respond to each method. Using the chart at the end of this chapter, you can estimate the probabilities of each response and note how much you would like each outcome. When you multiply your probability estimate by your style preference score, you will get a numerical score and can easily select the best approach to use—the one with the highest score.

For example, at a workshop, one man imagined the possible approaches and results in dealing with a conflict involving a close friend. He was disturbed that after a long, close friendship they appeared to be drifting apart. He felt that his friend had become self-centered and showed little interest in getting together, and he missed the many good times they shared together. Now Jim wasn't sure whether to discuss the problem with the friend, try to re-establish closer ties in other ways, or let the relationship drift away.

Before thinking about the possibilities, Jim needed to clarify the problem. Was this an isolated problem of drifting apart from this particular person, or did he experience this pattern with other people? If an isolated problem, Jim should consider a more targeted response to deal with this particular situation. However, if he noticed a series of similar conflicts in his life, he might need to make broader changes, perhaps in himself and his general approach to friendships.

After some thought, Jim concluded this was a particularized situation, involving his relationship with Bob. His next step was to focus on what he could or wanted to do. For Jim, a key concern was that he had let the relationship become unsatisfying for so long that he felt funny about even raising the subject with Bob. At the same time, he felt if he didn't say anything, they might continue to drift apart, and he didn't want that.

It was time for Jim to examine his alternatives and the likely outcomes of each approach. In the workshop, the other participants helped Jim think about the different approaches and the results, just as you might do on your own. You have to list the various alternatives to your problem and think about the likely results of each. Then, you rate these alternatives using a five-point scale, with 1 for extremely undesirable and 5 for most desirable, and 3 for average or neutral.

For example, in the ensuing discussion, Jim considered various possibilities:

- Saying nothing, which is a form of *accommodating* or giving in to the situation as it existed, so the relationship would continue to drift apart.

- Ending the relationship himself because he felt dissatisfied, a way of *avoiding* the situation by cutting it off himself.

- Saying something to try to repair the relationship and bring it back to where it used to be, by discussing the subject if his friend was receptive, which would be a form of *compromise* or *collaboration*, depending on how extensive the discussion was.

- Since the *competitive/confrontational* style wasn't appropriate for seeking to restore a mutual friendship, he didn't even consider this.

In assessing these possibilities, Jim was asked to consider a number of questions, such as how valuable the relationship was to him, and he used the chart to help him decide. If he felt it was worth it to try to get the relationship back to the way it was, it might be worth having a discussion with his friend. If he didn't feel it was worth it, he was urged to let it go, and to feel okay about doing that by realizing that relationships can grow and change, so even with a very good relationship it sometimes becomes appropriate to let the relationship go, because you have developed different concerns.

An example of how Jim used the chart is shown on the next page. It helped him decide that it was worth discussing his relationship with his friend in the hopes of saving it. Similarly, you can use the chart to help you come up with your own alternatives to the conflicts you face (see page 145).

Once you select an alternative, think about the best way to make it work. Jim, for example, after deciding to make a last attempt to restore his close friendship, decided to use an in-depth collaborative approach. But since he wasn't sure of the best way to raise the topic, he decided to go over what he planned to say and get input from others in the

Mapping Out Possibilities

Description of the Conflict: _I feel a formerly good relationship is breaking up and I'd like to keep this relationship if possible_

Is this a one-time conflict? ✔

a recurring conflict? _____

Rating Scale: 1 = least probable/desirable
3 = average probability/neutral desirability
5 = most probable/desirable

Possible Approaches (describe in detail)	Possible Outcomes Using That Style	Probability of Response (1–5)	Desirability of Outcome (1–5)	Score (Probability × Desirability)
Avoidance: ending the relationship now	immediate end of the relationship	5	1	5
Accommodation: letting things drift as is	gradual end of the relationship	3	2	6
Competition: not applicable	—	—	—	—
Compromise: talking about how we have some good times in the past and how it would be nice to continue the friendship	relationship will end anyway or relationship will be patched up and continue	3 3	2 3	6 9
Collaboration: exploring in-depth advantages of the relationship and how it could be mutually satisfying	relationship will end anyway or relationship will be patched up and continue	3 3	3 4	6 12

workshop. The result was that he got a series of suggestions about what to do, including letting his friend know he had some concerns he hoped to discuss, if his friend was willing to discuss them, and suggesting they go out for coffee or dinner to discuss them. Additionally, he was urged to keep the conversation casual, as well as to note how much he valued their friendship and the many things they had done together. Having created a supportive context, he then might ask his friend if something might have happened in his life so he wasn't able to respond to his calls as before. He was also reminded to: "Avoid sounding like you are accusing the person, recognize that your friend may have a different perspective on what has happened, and make it clear that you want to understand it and work things out." Finally, Jim was advised, "If your friend wants to talk about it and work out a resolution, fine. But if not, you should let the relationship go, knowing you at least tried to do what you could."

Likewise, you might spend some time imagining what you'll say or do in advance or get some suggestions from others, so you are be better prepared when you actually do it.

Take some time to become familiar with these different conflict styles and how to apply them as appropriate. As you become familiar with and learn to use these styles on a regular basis, you will find you can use them automatically in response to many conflicts. You will come to know which ones to use, as if by second nature.

In dealing with more serious, complex, or ongoing conflicts, such as those described in this chapter, you may want to use more specialized conflict techniques: visualization or mapping out the possibilities. With time, these will also come easily to you.

Mapping Out Possibilities

Description of the Conflict:

Is this a one-time conflict? _____

a recurring conflict? _____

Rating Scale:
1 = least probable/desirable
3 = average probability/neutral desirability
5 = most probable/desirable

Possible Approaches (describe in detail)	Possible Outcomes Using That Style	Probability of Response (1–5)	Desirability of Outcome (1–5)	Score (Probability × Desirability)
Avoidance:				
Accommodation:				
Competition:				
Compromise:				
Collaboration:				

11

Negotiating Win-Win
Solutions

Once you decide a conflict is worth resolving without avoiding it (avoidance), giving in to what someone else wants (accommodating), or forcing through your own resolution because you have the power (confrontation), you are left with a problem to work out through negotiation. You have to find the common ground between your desired solution and that of the other party.

The two ways of negotiating are through compromise or collaboration. These two approaches are similar in that they both involve back-and-forth give-and-take in working towards a solution that gives everyone some of what he or she wants. And ideally, you want to seek a win-win solution for all parties when using either approach. The major difference is that compromise focuses on surface issues and wants, while collaboration strives to go deeper.

In compromise, both parties begin by outlining their positions, or at least what they think they want. Then, each party begins making concessions and considering counteroffers, until an agreement is reached somewhere in the center. This is a common approach in settling money matters, (e.g., haggling over a price or negotiating a fair salary).

In collaboration, you go beyond the initial positions to look at the underlying interests, needs, and concerns of the parties. It can take some time and some digging for these to come to light. But the effort to explore these issues is part of the collaborative process, since a satisfactory solution takes all these factors into consideration. Using this approach resolves each party's concerns more thoroughly than a compromise. Collaboration takes more time and energy than most other conflict handling styles, but it often provides the best chance for forging a win-win solution.

In Chapter 9, I discussed and compared these two styles in detail if you want to further review them.

When to Use Compromise or Collaboration

So how do you know which method—compromise or collaboration—would be most appropriate? As with choosing any conflict resolution approach, the key is to take into consideration the specific circumstances surrounding the conflict, and to remain aware and flexible as negotiations proceed.

Generally, in certain circumstances, compromise is especially useful; in other circumstances, collaboration may be best.

Choose compromise when:

• The issues are relatively simple and clear-cut.

• There isn't much time to reach a solution or you want to achieve a resolution as quickly as possible.

• It would be better to achieve a temporary agreement quickly and deal with the more serious or underlying issues later.

• You and the other party (or parties) in the negotiation aren't very concerned about the goals or outcome of conflict.

• You haven't been able to resolve the matter using collaboration, or you haven't been able to get your way by using your own power to force a solution.

Choose collaboration when:

• The issues are fairly complex and require a detailed discussion to work out a solution acceptable to both parties.

• Both parties are willing to spend the time needed to deal with the underlying needs and concerns.

• Both parties feel their concerns are very important and don't want to compromise them.

- Both parties are willing to be open-minded and approach the negotiation in a spirit of good faith, which includes being willing to listen to and understand the other's concerns.

- Both parties want to achieve a permanent agreement, rather than a quick temporary solution, and are willing to deal with the issue now.

Why Win-Win Solutions Are Possible

Win-win solutions are possible because most conflicts stem from numerous causes. Initially, the conflict may appear to be rooted in two irreconcilable positions, and it may seem that both parties are emotionally invested in their opposing positions. But usually the parties are involved in the conflict for more than one reason due to their underlying interests or needs, and they attach different priorities to these reasons. As a result, several possible positions can satisfy a particular need.

Thus, the key to resolving a conflict the win-win way is to recognize and satisfy as best as possible each person's highest priorities or most important needs in return for getting concessions on lower priority items or needs. This is much like what happens in politics, as politicians bargain their support for one bill in return for someone else's support for their own pet project.

Experts in negotiation accordingly look for underlying reasons, interests, or needs and priorities when called in to settle disputes. Once these factors are identified, mediators encourage one party to give in on areas of lower priority in return for concessions to satisfy higher priority desires. Or mediators try to help disputants find new alternative positions that provide good payoffs for both. Such exchanges of concessions or new creative possibilities can be the key to a win-win solution.

As Fred E. Jandt, leader of conflict management seminars for professionals in business and public service, and author of *Win-Win Negotiating* (Hoboken, New Jersey: John Wiley & Sons, 1987), puts it: "One of the most effective techniques in conflict management is to identify all the sources of a particular conflict and to persuade the parties to compromise some in order to obtain concessions on others . . . There is never *only one* source of conflict . . . Inevitably, inescapably, and invariably, there will always be at least one secondary source."

Using this trade-off approach in negotiations, here are six steps to follow. Step 1 corresponds to the "E" in the E-R-I model (get the emotions under control); Steps 2 through 4 correspond to the "R" (use your reason to work towards a solution); and Steps 5 and 6 involve combining the "I" (use your intuition to come up with alternatives) with "R" to decide the best choice for you.

Step 1: Get the Emotions Under Control

Before you can identify the underlying sources and multiple interests in a conflict and look beneath the surface of your own and others' expressed positions, everybody has to get his or her emotions under control. The emotions have to be controlled so you can reasonably and rationally explore these underlying interests, concerns, reasons, and needs. Here's how.

If emotions are high on either side, take it upon yourself to begin work on clearing the air. It might not be possible to resolve all those feelings of anger, hurt, or resentment at once, but it is crucial they at least be diffused or set aside. Only then can you both deal calmly with the problem. Get your own emotions under control and appeal to the other party to do the same.

For example, you might say something like: "I know you're angry. I've been feeling that way myself. But if we're going to resolve this, we have to put our feelings aside and try to work on some alternatives. Would you be willing to do that?"

If the person still isn't ready to put feelings aside, you might say something like: "I know you're still very angry, and I'd like to understand why you feel that way. Maybe we can talk about the misunderstandings that caused this problem and then decide what we can do about it." This way you let the person know you want to deal with the problem and are willing to put any emotions aside to do this.

This "put-it-aside" approach doesn't mean denying all those feelings; rather, you are trying to acknowledge those feelings and put them in perspective so they don't interfere with achieving a resolution. A good way to use this approach is to allow each of you a little time to vent about how you feel. Then, once you have both vented the main issues and the venting seems to be rehashing old ground, suggest you might both try to work towards a resolution and that achieving this might itself help to get rid of any remaining anger or resentment. If the person still feels it necessary to vent again, you can stop and take time to revisit those feelings. But now, you hope you can both move on. If the other person has calmed down in response to your calmness and recognizes the logic of working on the resolution now, you'll be able to do so. In short, your focus should be on releasing the emotions and moving on; don't get stuck in going over the feelings and reasons for them.

If these initial efforts to diffuse emotions don't work because of the emotional intensity surrounding the conflict, take additional time to work on these emotions before going on. Refer to Section Two for a more detailed discussion on dealing with emotional issues.

Step 2: Agree on the Ground Rules

It helps to set up some ground rules in the beginning negotiation phase, especially if emotions have been high or if you are trying to resolve things with someone unfamiliar with the negotiation process. Take the lead, if you can. Explain that the ground rules are designed to keep the process going smoothly.

Some of the basic rules to suggest that you agree to include:

- Listen to each other as carefully as you can.
- Do not interrupt each other.
- Do not get angry or express hostility even if one of you disagrees with something the other says.
- Treat each other with respect.
- Establish the amount of time you want to devote to the process—and stick to it.
- Try to see the other's point of view.

Such rules are normally set forth by mediators and local conflict resolution groups at the beginning of their negotiation sessions to help the parties discuss and resolve their disputes. The rules set a tone of mutual respect and fair play, and help set the stage for productive negotiation. Similar rules can achieve the same effect for you.

Once you've laid out ground rules, you can always refer to them if the negotiation process breaks down or tempers start rising. Such a breakdown in the process is a signal to call time out and refocus everyone back on the goal of the negotiation. You might say something like: "I know you're feeling really angry. But we agreed we would try to listen to each other and treat each other with respect. If you can let me finish what I was trying to say, then I'd like to listen to you."

For maximum effectiveness, get the other person's agreement when you set the rules, as well as any suggestions for additional rules. Usually it will be easy to agree, since you are merely suggesting rules of ordinary human courtesy and respect. If you can't come to an agreement, that could be a sign that the feelings underlying the conflict run too deep. Or perhaps this lack of agreement may indicate that the other party is not coming from a place of good will—a barrier to a successful outcome, because both parties need to negotiate in a spirit of good faith for a mutually satisfying result. If you think that the other person is not showing good will, consider alternative approaches to resolution: avoidance, accommodation, or forcing your way through if you have the power to do this. But if you still think there are hopes for negotiation, return to Step 1.

Step 3: Clarify Your Positions

Once the emotional thicket is trimmed down and rules are set, the first phase of the actual negotiation is a chance to get all the issues, opinions, positions, and views out in the open. If the other person is willing to put everything out on the table, expect to express your own concerns, too.

But before stating your positions in detail, find out where the other person is coming from, and what he or she perceives, wants, and needs. When you take that person's desires and concerns into consideration, it will help you shape your own proposals. You'll still seek to gain what you most want. But you'll help the other person feel heard and understood, and in doing so you'll improve your chances of being received in a positive way and gaining a more favorable outcome for yourself.

Here are some guidelines for understanding the other's position.

1. **Look at the world from the other person's point of view.** Try to step into the other's shoes for a while, so you can imagine what that person is thinking or perceiving. This can help you in assessing what he or she thinks is important, what he or she is willing or not willing to give up, what he or she fears, and so forth. You don't have to agree with this point of view, but you need to understand it. The empathy will improve your rapport as you negotiate, and it will even help you in influencing the other person to accept an agreement. After all, if you seem to understand where he or she is coming from, he or she will trust you more.

2. **Avoid making judgments about what the other person thinks, believes, or has done.** Sure, you may think you are right. The other person probably thinks he or she is right, too. Even if the other person is clearly wrong, he or she may not want to admit it to you (or to him- or herself). As a general rule, it is not helpful to start criticizing or blaming the other person, even if the other person did make a mistake. It will just make the other person defensive and resistant to you or your ideas. That person may start criticizing or blaming *you* to feel better or to even the score, and negotiations are likely to give way to heated exchanges and hurt feelings.

What do you do if the other party starts blaming or criticizing you? Try not to jump at the bait and attack or get defensive in kind. Just keep in mind your goal of seeking to negotiate some resolution for the future, and try to move as quickly as possible toward that. If you can, refer back to the rule you set about not expressing hostility.

3. **Discuss any differences in perceptions, assumptions, and beliefs.** Since differences in outlook and interpretation can be a major block to negotiating an agreement, get them out in the open to correct them. If, for example, someone assumes you agreed to do something you never did, that belief might lead the person to think you are irresponsible and to distrust your attempts to guide the negotiation process. So, to alter that person's wrong impression, make it clear what really happened (e.g., you never agreed). Do so in a way that allows the other person to accept the fact that his or her perception was incorrect. You don't want to accuse or blame the other person for being wrong. Rather, point out that you both may have different perceptions, assumptions, or beliefs, and that you want to clear up any confusions. Sometimes just bringing these perceptions, assumptions, and beliefs out in the open is enough to clarify matters.

Discussing any differences of understanding in this open, nonthreatening way makes it easier for either of you to acknowledge any incorrect perceptions and assumptions. Should you be correct about something, but the other person has difficulty recognizing his or her mistakes, it may be because the other person has difficulty acknowledging being wrong or needs more convincing of your viewpoint. If the former, try to find a diplomatic, face-saving way for the person to gracefully retreat from a position; if the latter, offer to provide proof of your assertions if you can, such as with letters, documents, or a third party to corroborate your story.

4. **Involve the other person in the negotiation process even though you take the lead.** Even if you take the initiative and suggest most of the ideas, let the other party feel he or she has contributed valuable ideas, so he or she feels more of a stake in the resolution. To this end, during the negotiation, encourage the other person to contribute suggestions on ways of working out the problem. If you can, frame your ideas so that they tie in with something the other person has said or with what you perceive is the other person's way of thinking. And if the other person proposes what you want or have already said, by all means let the person think it's his or her great idea. People are generally more willing to carry out ideas they see as their own, and then you get what you want, too. That's the essence of a true win-win solution.

5. **Keep your initial bargaining position reasonable and realistic.** Sometimes there's a tendency to start off with an extreme position, based on the notion that you'll each come down a little and meet somewhere in the middle. In traditional negotiations, starting off with a higher position can result in a better outcome for you than starting off low. But if you go too high, you can appear unreasonable and lead the other person to respond in kind with a similarly extreme opposing position. You thus begin very far apart and instead of this approach leading to a neutral compromise in the middle, this distance can make it more difficult to achieve a resolution. It does so by interfering with a cooperative spirit and it can create a siege mentality for negotiation, where you are both adversaries, each trying to get the best of the other. By contrast, beginning with a more reasonable realistic position invites the other person to participate with you as a partner in your search for a resolution. This sets a tone of fairness, and makes it easier to achieve a resolution that works for you both.

And what if you begin reasonably and the other person takes advantage by coming on strong? Remain firm and point out that you want to find a solution that is fair to you both. Emphasize the reasonableness of your offer and explain your hope that the other person is willing to proceed in a spirit of fairness. It's a strong appeal, since people tend to have a sense of justice, and commonly the other person will come around.

Step 4: Explore Underlying Needs and Interests

Now, with the emotional blocks cleared out of the way, the ground rules stated, and the basic issues on the table, you are ready to focus on getting and giving information on what you each really want and need out from this negotiation. That means going beyond initially stated positions to explore underlying feelings and reasons for wanting what you want.

Here are some ways to proceed.

Ask Why the Other Person Chose That Position

You want to know why a person has done something or says he wants something, as well as what he needs, would like, expects, hopes for, is afraid of, or is concerned about in taking a particular position. By responding to those underlying needs, wants, expectations, hopes, fears, or concerns, you might be able to alter his or her position by coming up with some alternative method of achieving his goals.

As an example, imagine that the company you work for has a strict policy about workers coming to work and leaving at a certain time. You are working on a special project and feel you could do a better job working at home. But when you suggest it, your boss says, "No working at home, that's company policy." However, if you start probing, you may find the reasons for this policy are that the company is afraid that people will take advantage of more flexible rules by not working as hard and taking long breaks. Also, the company wants people on board so when clients call, the employees are there.

By knowing these underlying reasons, you can propose alternate choices that satisfy your boss, such as using time sheets at home to show time worked, offering to work extra hours for the commuting time saved, and proposing a few trial days to show how much extra work you can do. You have a better chance of getting your way by satisfying the other party that your alternate proposal works, and the result is you have found a win-win solution for you both.

When you ask these "why" questions about the other's position, ask them in a neutral, concerned way, so the person feels you really want to understand where he or she is coming from. Avoid sounding like a cross-examiner asking the person to explain or justify his position, which would only make the person defensive and even resentful that you sound so righteous.

Ask Why Your Position Was Not Chosen

Another way to probe for underlying needs and concerns is to learn why a person hasn't made the choice you consider most reasonable and desirable. Again, frame your question in a neutral way, so it doesn't sound like you are accusing the person. Instead of asking, "Why didn't you do _____?" ask "What were your reasons for choosing not to do _____? I'd really like to understand how you felt about this." You are asking for the same information, but your approach is more friendly and comfortable. It lets the person feel safe in answering on a topic where you disagree, because you are not challenging him to defend his answer.

Listen carefully to the answer you receive. You might recognize the blocks standing in the way of action or resolution and find ways to change the person's mind by helping to remove those blocks. Or perhaps the person's reasons for not choosing your position will sound reasonable, suggesting that you may not be able to achieve change in this area. So it might make more sense to try to change in the person's position with another proposed alternative—or perhaps even consider that person's preferred resolution.

For example, suppose you and a friend have a conflict about taking responsibility. Your friend promised to do something while you were away, but didn't—and didn't just forget, but decided he didn't *want* to do these things. But she didn't tell you that, so you only found out what happened later. Without accusing your friend of irresponsibility, you might try to find out why she decided not to act. Once you have made it clear that you are not upset and expressed real curiosity, your friend might feel comfortable telling you the real reasons, since you have created a safe space for opening up to you. Maybe she felt you were asking too much but didn't want to tell you that. As a result, she felt obligated to agree to do you a favor as a friend, but resented the pressure to say yes. So she just didn't do what she agreed, saying no with her actions. Once these real feeling are out in the open, you can deal with the expectations and limits of your friendship, not whether your friend did or didn't do some task.

Getting to that point requires careful questioning and listening, and a willingness to be open and honest yourself.

Probe for Multiple Interests

Normally, both you and the other party will have more than one reason for holding a position. If more than one party is on the other side, the different individuals may have a variety of motivating reasons. Get all of these reasons out in the open, and share your reasons as well.

Use the methods of neutral questioning and active listening previously described to ferret out the various underlying reasons. Show your concern for the other party to set the stage for a calm exchange of ideas and to help make the other party more receptive to listening to your own concerns. When you do find one plausible idea that may be doable, don't stop—there may be more. Acknowledge the idea and ask if there's anything else.

If the other person seems uncertain, suggest additional possible issues yourself to encourage further digging. Point out that often people have multiple interests and you do, too, so it would be helpful to share them. That way, by all of you putting your multiple interests on the table, you can see if there are areas of mutual agreement or complementary concerns, so all parties can be better able to gain from negotiation.

Once you know all the reasons and concerns and show you acknowledge and understand them, you can then learn which ones are most important to the other person. By discovering relative priorities, you have a basis for proposing some trade-offs. Compare the other party's priorities to yours. Then, try to find a way to get each of your most important needs met, while making concessions on the others.

If you find it confusing to keep all the multiple needs straight, particularly in a complex group conflict, make a list and write down who wants what either during or after your discussion. Then, go over this list and note priorities. Circle the most important needs. If it's a long list, underline the second most important needs. As you rank the relative importance of these needs to the parties to the conflict, the points on which you can negotiate should become clearer.

Talk about Your Own Interests and Needs

Since satisfying your own needs as well as others' is important, make your needs known also, as is appropriate. Make them specific and concrete, even vivid in your descriptions, so the other side can clearly see and empathize with your problem.

For instance, if you are having a dispute with an employer over a long-postponed raise, give some compelling reasons why your salary now feels inadequate. When you do so, first obtain your employer's agreement to listen and be sure to show your concern about meeting his needs (such as pointing out how this raise will benefit him by making you a more motivated, committed, productive worker).

While it can be fine to point up your own needs for a particular result, emphasize what the other person would gain from meeting your needs. For example, you might mention needing a promised raise to pay back a loan or enroll in an evening MA program. But then use specifics to make your needs come to life for the listener, showing how you recognize the other side's needs and concerns, too. One way to do this is to preface a discussion of your needs by summarizing your understanding of what the other party wants. In the raise scenario described above, you might say something like: "I realize the company has had to keep costs down because of increased competition. That's why I've been working on improving efficiency over the past couple of years." As you present arguments for why you deserve more money, give specifics on what you have done and what you are worth. Make your perspective clear and compelling, and make your interests sound like they are in the other party's interest, too. If you can get your listener to sympathize and agree—through vivid detail—this can help you reach an agreement you want.

It's often a good idea to explain your reasons, interests, or needs before you state your position. That way, the other person is more receptive to listening, because you have provided a meaningful context or rationale. If you start with your position, the other party may block it out or become defensive upon seeing that your position directly opposes his own. In this case, he wants to guard against your implementing this different point of view, much like a guard in football running interference against an opposing team. But if you begin by being very clear about your reasons for feeling as you do or wanting what you want, this helps the other party see things from your point of view and to be more receptive to what you are saying.

As another example, consider a husband-wife scenario. The wife has been staying home to take care of the young kids, while the husband works in a factory. She now wants to put her children in a day-care facility and return to work. Yet she knows this will anger her husband, since he may feel threatened by her independence and worry about the kids staying with strangers. If she tells him her desired position immediately, she fears this will provoke an uproar because he will immediately resist. By contrast, suppose she eases into her point of view—perhaps talking in general about how nice it would be to have some more time and money to enjoy the things they like together, while helping the kids have more contact with other children. This might help her husband hear and consider the reasonableness of her proposal. It might also give him the space and inclination to share his own needs in a productive, amicable way. In turn, this calm exchange means that an emotional argument will be less likely.

Thus generally sharing your reasoning before stating a position—and making that reasoning detailed and vivid—is a good way to open up the door to a solution that works for you both. It helps you keep things calm, humanizes you, shows the reasonableness of your position, and thereby helps the other person be open to seeing things from your point of view.

Step 5: Generate Alternatives

Once you have a clear idea of what both parties want—having shared your interests and needs and listened to the other person's—you are ready for the next phase of the negotiation: coming up with alternatives to meet these needs. You can try brainstorming alternatives with the other party. Or do some brainstorming on your own and present your best options to the other party later. You'll find more details on brainstorming to generate alternatives in Chapter 13. Here are some basic considerations to keep in mind:

Suspend Judgment: Quantity Counts More than Quality

Initially, come up with as many possibilities as you can. Don't try to evaluate or critique them yet; this will inhibit the creative flow. Offer suggestions yourself and invite suggestions from the other party or parties. Emphasize that you want to look at all the possible options now and don't want to make any decisions about them until later. Tell people that even "crazy" or "impossible" ideas are welcome. And it doesn't matter who comes up with what ideas, since there's no judging and no person will be associated with any particular idea. Then everyone feels freer. Tell them that as ideas come up, you or someone else will write them down so everyone can see them.

Later, when you have a long list of ideas to choose from, you can go over them and decide which ones might be workable—individually and in combinations with other ideas. You might think of the various options as trading cards with different values. You can choose which cards to put on the table, look at counteroffers contained in other people's cards, and eventually reach an agreement on which cards should remain up for discussion. If you have trouble deciding which cards everyone thinks should remain on the table, first decide which cards nobody wants at all and eliminate unworkable possibilities by discarding those cards. Afterwards, with the pool of options more manageable in size, you can better scrutinize and play with each card. Ultimately, narrow the pile down to the cards everyone feels can create a win-win solution that works for everybody.

Focus on the Future

Sometimes, even after you have dealt with emotions and talked about everybody's reasons and needs, the temptation to express emotions and present explanations and justifications again can be inviting. Resist this urge. Don't waste energy and poison a productive atmosphere by rehashing the past. If somebody begins to do this, gently interrupt. Indicate that you appreciate his or her feelings—provide some acknowledgement and reassurance. Then, provide another reminder that your focus should be on resolving the conflict for the future, not on what caused it in the past.

Remain Open to Different Alternatives

While it is helpful to have a sense of where you want to go in a negotiation, it's critical to remain open to other ideas—both those you come up with and those offered by the other person. The key to finding a resolution that will satisfy your underlying needs or interests as well as the other person's is staying flexible. Remember that there are many possibilities in each problem situation. Allow yourself to consider all the options and avoid prematurely squelching or criticizing ideas you consider wrong or crazy. Others may disagree—and their ideas just may work.

Avoid Closing Off Possibilities Too Quickly

As you think about possible options, you may be tempted to reach a quick resolution and settle for the first reasonable alternative. This can be fine if all parties feel really comfortable with this outcome. But if you sense any doubts or feel that the resolution was reached too quickly for people to be comfortable with it, take the time to explore other options.

One reason for this tendency to jump at an early solution is that it can be hard to come up with options. That's because, as Fisher and Ury explain in *Getting to Yes*: "Inventing options does not come naturally. *Not inventing is the normal state of affairs.*" Moreover, people commonly see their task as "narrowing the gap between positions, not broadening the options available." They tend to think: "We're having a hard enough time agreeing as it is. The last thing we need is a bunch of different ideas." People tend to hold this narrow approach, since they hope for a single decision to result from the negotiation and feel an expanded discussion of options will only delay and confuse things.

The truth is that an open discussion of alternatives can uncover a really good solution that all parties feel comfortable with. It may take a little longer to reach this decision, but if the issue is truly important or complex, it may be worth it. Try to convince others of this fact, and keep your discussion going until you feel people have stretched their imaginations to consider new possibilities. Occasionally, the first proposal may be so terrific that you all want to accept it instantly. If so, fine. But normally, it's a good idea to keep the channels open for a while so you come up with even more ideas and choose the optimum one, not the first reasonable option.

Step 6: Agree on the Best Win-Win Options

As you propose solutions with a payoff for you, describe the payoffs for the other person to show you want this to be a win-win for everyone. The other person will see you care and be apt to respond in kind. This approach will also help you come up with win-win options in what you propose, while recognizing the ones that don't hold win-win potential.

The advantage of this approach is you don't view the negotiation as a zero-sum, you win/I lose type of game. In a conflict, you aren't dealing with a limited universe, in which a gain for one person is a loss for the other. That might occur in a straight buyer-seller situation, where the more the seller charges, the more the buyer pays. But in resolving conflict, gains can occur on a number of levels, because people bring to a negotiation multiple interests and needs. For instance, if an employee gives up salary benefits in return for a better position in the company, that could be a gain both for the employee (in terms of status and pride) and for the company (especially if it's experiencing tight times and needs to cut back financially).

Help the Other Party Feel Comfortable Making Concessions

As you suggest possibilities or encourage the other person to think of alternatives, you may encounter some resistance. If this occurs, it may be because the other person is viewing the changes from an initial position as concessions or losses. Sometimes it's enough to emphasize that you're using the negotiation to find a mutually agreeable solution. But when these resistances occur, you may need to do more.

One approach to overcome resistance or keep it from occurring is to make it as comfortable as possible for the other person to let go of certain points. The person should feel he or she is really gaining something in return for what he or she is giving up, or that these concessions will lead to a satisfying end result. Let the person save face and maintain a high self-image and self-esteem. It's a small concession for you to make to gain a bargaining outcome in your favor. Don't let the other party feel his or her image was diminished by giving in on a particular point.

One way to make the person feel good about backing off from a position is to praise the person for any concessions. Let him know he's done something good or noble and that he's making the negotiation process work. You want to acknowledge and support the other party where you can and avoid any blaming or shaming. (Don't go overboard or your praise will seem phony.) Thus, to show your support without shame or blame, don't accuse the other person of being wrong or slow to admit responsibility for what he did—and don't gloat when something seems to be turning your way. Rather, it's best to emphasize that you understand any difficulties the other person may be having in dealing with this difficult issue and that you really appreciate what the person is doing. And when things are going well for both of you, let the other person know—reinforce the potential for mutual success.

This strategy of providing positive support for concessions saved the day at one conflict resolution panel. A teenage boy had borrowed a coat from a friend, and soon afterwards a neighborhood tough had taken the coat from him. The boy kept promising to get the coat back from the boy who took it, but he was unable to get it. The case finally ended up before a panel, because the coat's original owner wanted it back or wanted the boy who took it to reimburse him. For a long time, as the panel continued, the boy kept talking vaguely about his hopes of retrieving the coat. Only after it became apparent he had no realistic chance of getting the coat did he finally and painfully admit that, yes, he was responsible and agreed to reimburse his friend for the cost of the coat. And with that he slumped in his seat like a deflated balloon, having made a very difficult concession. But then, by praising him and supporting him for what he had done, the entire panel helped him feel better. Though he had given something up, he got back his pride. As a result, the two boys walked out of the session still friends.

Another way to help a person feel better about a concession is to build up what the person is getting in return. For example, she is giving up a room with a view, but her new office will be larger and closer to the office machines she regularly uses.

You'll also make the person feel much better if you can match a concession he or she makes with one of your own. Even a minor point offered can reinforce the collaborative spirit. If you have nothing to offer or it's inappropriate for you to concede anything more, be sure to express your appreciation. Point out that the person's concession is bringing both of you closer to a mutually satisfying solution.

Summing Up

In short, the E-R-I model proposed in this book can be readily adapted to be used in a negotiation.

- You start by dealing with emotions to get them out of the way.
- Next, using your reason, you listen actively to the needs and reasons of the other person, showing that you have really heard and understood them. Next, you share your own reasons and needs, describing them as vividly and fairly as you can.
- Then, you move into the intuitive phase, where you throw out as many options as possible.
- Finally, using a combination of your reason and intuition, you evaluate these proposed options later, choosing among them to come up with a resolution that provides some satisfaction for all parties involved.

As you follow these steps, your conflict will be resolved, and each party will feel like a winner.

Learning to Deal with Difficult People

The conflict resolution strategies described in this book are designed to work with most people under most everyday situations. But some especially difficult people with certain personality characteristics require special handling to resolve a problem. These people are often apt to push your buttons and infuriate you, and they are frequently highly emotional themselves. You have to be especially careful to not let them get to you. Besides using the basic principles already discussed, you can use specific strategies to deal with some commonly identified categories of difficult people.

Who Are These Difficult People?

Exactly who you consider a very difficult person to deal with can vary, based on your own personality traits and past experiences, since one person's difficult person may not always be difficult for someone else to deal with—though, of course, some people are hard for anyone to deal with.

For example, a woman who has suffered as a child from an overprotective, possessive mother may find any strong, overbearing authority figure (particularly female) a difficult person to deal with. However, a man who served in the armed forces and likes a strong commanding figure telling him what to do may not find that person difficult at all. Or a man who has divorced his nagging wife—a stickler for neatness—after a long courtroom battle may feel that anyone who seems like a perfectionist is someone who presents difficulties, whereas other people may like being with or working for someone who sets a high standard for excellence.

Apart from these special reasons for finding someone difficult, there are certain types of widely acknowledged "difficult" people, according to counselors, therapists, employers, researchers, and others who work or live with them. Keep in mind, though, that these people may be difficult in some situations but not in others. For instance, the guy who is a tyrant at home may be a lamb in the workplace, or vice versa.

Descriptions of these people make the process of dealing with difficult people a little like bird watching. First, identify the personality type; afterwards, can categorize and find tips on what to do to deal with that particular type of person.

In Robert M. Bramson's classic *Coping with Difficult People* (New York: Ballantine Books, 1981) the author identifies about a dozen different types, based on thirty years of experience working with public and private organizations. These difficult types include:

- *Hostile-Aggressives,* divided up into "Sherman tanks," "Snipers," and "Exploders." These are people who (respectively) try to bully others to get their way, make underhanded cutting remarks, or throw temper tantrums if no one listens.

- *Complainers,* who always have something to gripe about. However, they generally don't do anything to resolve the problem, because they feel powerless to do anything or don't want to take the responsibility.

- *Clams,* who are silent and unresponsive. You don't know what they really think or want.

- *Super-Agreeables,* who eagerly say yes to just about everything and appear to offer you support. But they don't follow through to produce what they say they will, or they act differently than they lead you to expect.

- *Naysayers* and *Perennial Pessimists,* who find a reason why anything suggested won't work. Since they usually think things will go wrong, they tend to say no most of the time or worry constantly after saying yes.

- *Know-It-All Experts,* who act superior to everyone else because they think they know everything and want everyone else to know it. They may come across like "bulldozers," who push others out of the way with their knowledge. Or they may be more like "balloons," who are overinflated with their own knowledge and importance—and are often wrong.

- *Indecisives* and *Stallers,* who have trouble making decisions because they are afraid of being wrong or not perfect. So they wait until the decision is made for them or the need to make the decision is over.

Other difficult people include those who set up expectations, but act contrary to them. Psychotherapist Dr. George R. Bach, in his and co-author Ronald M. Deutsch's book, *Stop! You're Driving Me Crazy* (New York: Berkeley Books, 1979), calls them "crazymakers." They make people crazy by setting up the belief that a person or thing will perform a certain way, although the expected doesn't happen. As a result, their behavior breaks down the fundamental trust that must exist between people to smooth their interactions. Still other types of crazymakers set up contradictory expectations and expect you to meet them. Sometimes a crazymaker may ask you to do something, but then sets up obstacles or otherwise sabotages your ability to achieve your goal, so you fail.

You can probably think of many other people whose personality styles make them difficult to deal with. Possibly, they will be variations on some of these basic types, or you may find additional categories, such as:

- The *Perfectionist*—the overly rigid person who wants everything just so, even when it may not be necessary or preferable to do so.

- The *Secret Fort*—the person who keeps everything in, won't tell you what's wrong, and suddenly attacks you when you think everything is fine.

- The *Innocent Liar*—the person who covers his or her tracks with a lie or a series of lies, so you end up not knowing what to trust or believe.

- The *Resentful Altruist*—the person who appears to be helpful and giving, but under the surface, begrudges what he or she gives. Sometimes this resentment may percolate to the surface in other encounters or it may be expressed nonverbally through unexpected sabotage or withdrawal.

Additionally, there are the many Game Players, such as the "yes, but-er," described by Eric Berne in his book *The Games People Play* (New York: Grove Press, 1964). A "yes, but-er" is a person who acts one way on the surface, while concealing some other hidden agenda. You don't know what's going on until you fall into their trap, like a bug flying in and out of a Venus' flytrap. At some point your wings will brush the edges of the game-playing person and the trap will close.

Your own list probably contains several other difficult types. But identifying a type is just the first step. You need to know what to *do* when you interact with someone on your list.

Some General Principles for Dealing with Difficult People

A good general principle to keep in mind in dealing with any difficult person: Most people are difficult because they have certain underlying needs or interests that they meet by acting the way they do. The super-aggressive person may act like a Steamroller because underneath he is afraid of dealing with people or confronting the fear that he may be wrong. The silent Clam may play it close to the vest because she is afraid of revealing herself to others. The Perennial Pessimist may always think things will go wrong because it is more comfortable to live with the certainty of failure than the uncertainty of hoping and finding those hopes unfulfilled—and this attitude contributes to the many failures the Pessimist experiences.

Thus, if you deal with any people you consider difficult, look for their underlying needs and think of how you can satisfy them. It's the same approach as taking an individual's needs into consideration in an everyday conflict situation. In addition, take into consideration other principles and strategies outlined in this book. Think how they might apply to the particular situation you are in and adapt them to dealing with the particular type of difficult person.

Work Through the Emotional Charges Triggered by a Difficult Person

Not only can dealing with a difficult person make you upset, angry, frustrated, depressed, or otherwise put you emotionally off-center, but the difficult person may be emotionally charged, too, like the Exploder who throws a temper tantrum to get his or her way. Thus, as in any conflict situation, a first step is getting your own emotions under control or helping the other person blow off his or her emotions, though these may be more intense than usual because this is a difficult person.

You can refer to Chapter 2 and the chapters in Section Two for more specific details on dealing with emotions. Here are a few more points to keep in mind:

• Don't take the other person's behavior personally. A difficult person is likely to use the same kinds of dysfunctional behavior with everybody to satisfy his or her needs. Remind yourself of this to help you avoid any feelings of self-blame and to feel less upset yourself.

• Notice if you are finding this person difficult because he or she reminds you of someone with whom you have had previous bad experiences. For example, does this person remind you of your overprotective mother? Your older brother who is always ready with a putdown? Your perfectionist ex-spouse?. If this person does trigger negative reminders, seek to separate your reactions to this person now from your reactions to that other person in the past by reminding yourself this person is not the person from your past.

• Use creative visualization, affirmations, or other calming techniques to cool yourself down and release your emotions.

• Listen without judgment to let the other person release some of his or her emotions.

• If you become emotionally upset because you are picking up the difficult person's way of viewing the world (i.e., you are beginning to feel down because you are with a Perennial Pessimist or hostile because you are with a Hostile-Aggressive person), notice that you are doing this, so you can stop yourself. Remind yourself that you are letting yourself see things from another person's point of view, and while you are open to understanding this view, you are not that person; you have your own viewpoint. So distance yourself from the other person by repeating to yourself again and again, "I am not that person. I have my own way of seeing the world," or some such statement. As you do, breathe out and let go. Imagine yourself letting go of that person's point of view and retrieving your own.

Think about Why the Difficult Person Is Being Difficult

It can help you make the difficult person less difficult if you think about what that person may need or want that is leading him or her to be difficult. Maybe you can undermine the source of that person becoming difficult. To this end, ask yourself: What are that person's goals, and how is being difficult helping to achieve that end? By assessing the person's needs, you can better decide if you want to address them. You may have to if that person is in a higher power position than you (such as your boss) and you don't want to leave your own position. Or this needs assessment might convince you that you don't want to deal with the situation at all. You can then walk away from it more knowledgeably than if you just decided to tune out, knowing only about the situation and little about the personal dynamics of the other person involved in the conflict.

For example, say you are confronted by a silent Clam with whom you've been friends for years, but now he seems very distant. When you see each other, you feel this person doesn't want to talk to you. But why? You feel something may have happened to affect your relationship, but aren't sure what and you're feeling increasingly angry and frustrated. One approach might be simply to say "forget it," and avoid the situation altogether. If the other person isn't going to tell you what's wrong, too bad. You're not going to play mind reader. You can walk away and go on with your life, which feels like the most comfortable thing to do.

On the other hand, you might hesitate to walk away if the person has been a valuable friend. Maybe she is seeking to avoid talking to you now because she is upset or embarrassed about something that has nothing to do with you. Or maybe this person is afraid to confront you with a complaint about what really is bothering him, because he feels it might be difficult to deal with the feelings released by the encounter.

Once you clarify that you do want to proceed, you might try to reach these underlying needs by showing you are eager to be supportive and nonjudgmental, and by encouraging the person to talk. Paying attention to needs isn't guaranteed to open the person up. But it is a direct and thoughtful approach, and the short time it takes might certainly prove worth the effort.

This method of probing for needs is of course useful in encounters with anyone; however, it is particularly helpful in dealing with a difficult person, since what makes a person difficult is these special needs. In everyday conflicts, people certainly are motivated by their needs. But often these needs are situational or motivated by common desires for prestige, belonging, achievement, and financial gain. With difficult people, needs are commonly more buried or more linked to past losses and frustrations (such as the superaggressive person who is trying to cover up underlying feelings of shyness, or the "yes, but-er" who is not used to success and questions his or her self-worth). You shouldn't play psychiatrist or may not want to. But if you at least offer the person a supportive, friendly listener, you may be able to help the person understand his or her own needs. You may even find the difficult person is suddenly not being difficult anymore, for he or she has found you to be someone to trust and cooperate with instead.

Using Communication to Get to the Root of the Difficulty

Frequently, people are difficult because communication gaps lead them to have wrong assumptions or misunderstandings about something, so they act out of fear or distrust. While communication problems can lead to conflict with anyone, with a difficult person these communication problems become even more serious. They become magnified because the difficult person tends to overreact, and a small obstacle becomes a mountain.

An example is a mixed-messages miscommunication at work that leads an employee to think a co-worker is trying to sabotage her own efforts and make her look bad to the supervisor. Since the midyear reviews are coming up, she thinks the other employee wants to increase his chances for a promotion. In an ordinary situation, the worker might get angry, confront the other employee with her suspicions, or perhaps engineer some reverse sabotage. The sparring back and forth might seem like office politics as usual.

However, in this kind of situation, the "difficult" person is apt to be much more sensitive to any perceived slights or attacks, and could respond even more intensely, creating a far more explosive situation. In fact, the difficult person might even use his reputation for being difficult to get his way and get others to back down. For instance, the Aggressive-Hostile might respond by an explosion of anger, threats, dire predictions, and heated accusations to intimidate others. Or the Clam might retreat even more into his shell, showing that he won't deign to speak to the employee he believes to be at the root of his problems.

Thus, with difficult people it can be especially critical to clear out the channels so the correct communications can go through. It may be harder to do this and you may have to put more effort into get your message across than with a nondifficult person (for example, by being more insistent, conciliatory, respectful, or solicitous). But if you really want to resolve the conflict, rather than just avoid dealing with it, it may be worth the attempt. You may be able to cut through the layer of emotional armor, distrust, and fear that makes the difficult person difficult in the first place. And once you do, you may find the difficult person is not so difficult anymore, at least with you.

Overcoming the Responsibility Trap with a Difficult Person

Difficult people can be particularly sensitive about issues of blame and responsibility. They may be more likely to seek to blame others, or more vociferous in their accusations. Or they may be more defensive if they think someone else is blaming them, and they may even act defensive if they think they really are at fault, but don't want to admit it to others or themselves. In fact, one difficult type is the *Chronic Blamer*, who is eager to find fault when something goes wrong and put the accusing finger on someone else. It's as if the Blamer sees blaming as the key to resolving the problem. But pointing fingers usually does no such thing, since beyond assigning responsibility, it puts down the person who has supposedly done the wrong, which just makes the person feel bad. He or she will probably respond with a correspondingly defensive response, e.g., "I didn't do it . . . she did," or "Maybe I did it, but I was only following orders."

The opposite of the Blamer is the *Martyr*, who wants to take the blame for something he didn't do or make his own wrongdoing seem even worse, as if this self-debasement will correct or atone for the problem. The Martyr often does this because he hopes that others will like or approve of him more, because he has taken on the scapegoat role. But that doesn't solve the underlying problem either.

The problem with both Martyr and Chronic Blamer is that they tend to dramatize and thereby escalate any conflict by overlaying the basic problem with their own personal needs. For example, the Blamer typically feels he must always be right and support this feeling by making others seem wrong. By contrast, the Martyr typically wants desperately to be liked, so he or she will step into the scapegoat role, so everyone else will feel relieved of the blame and have the Martyr to thank.

To make things worse, these two difficult types—the Martyr and the Blamer—combine this behavior with other types of difficult roles. For instance, the Hostile-Aggressive Steamroller or Exploder may easily become a Blamer and scream and blame everyone else, while the silent Clam may take on the Martyr role by letting everyone dump on him without saying anything to resist.

Thus, with a difficult person, it is especially important to avoid getting stuck in the responsibility trap (see Chapter 7). Try not to let the discussion focus on assigning responsibility for the problem. One way to do this might be to move away from discussing what happened and why in the past and move towards seeking for solutions in the future. You might say yes, this happened, and yes, you (or the other person, or perhaps still others) may have some responsibility for what occurred. But now that doesn't matter much. Now what's really important is focusing on what you can each do together to achieve a resolution.

In other words, neutralize the difficult person's concerns about past responsibility and take the initiative in directing the person's awareness toward the future. This strategy may seem to fly in the face of getting people to accept responsibility if they are at fault in order to get them to act to correct the problem. Also, it may seemingly contradict the importance of acknowledging responsibility when you recognize your own contribution to the conflict. But if you are dealing with a difficult person who is determined to blame others or take the blame, it may be better to deflect this urge by downplaying the importance of taking responsibility. Instead, stress the need to think about how to resolve the conflict now, regardless of who may have been responsible for it in the past. While you may ultimately get a Blamer to accept responsibility or a Martyr to let it go, you do so by sidestepping the issue with a focus on action in the present.

Choosing the Style of Conflict to Suit the Difficult Person

Considering the type of difficult person you are dealing can also help you choose the appropriate conflict style or combination of styles to use: competition/confrontation, accommodation, compromise, collaboration, or avoidance.

In dealing with a difficult person, avoidance may seem the ideal choice, because the person is so hard to deal with. You often want to walk away from the Blamer, Exploder, Steamroller, Perennial Pessimist, Complainer, or any of the other difficult types. But in many cases you can't do this. You might work with or for these people or a difficult person may have something you want or need.

For example, one time I was involved in a writing project with a Blamer, Complainer, and Perennial Pessimist. To some extent, these behaviors were triggered by a new project, since the man had never written a book before. He was constantly worried that things would go wrong, and he didn't trust me, the publisher, or the book industry generally, though he desperately wanted to have a book. So he seemed like a tinderbox ready to blow, and I felt like I was constantly walking on eggshells since almost anything could set him off. But I had made a commitment to finish the book, would get paid when I did, and the book already had been accepted by the man's prospective publisher. So I found ways to calm him down, reassure him, and acknowledge his fears and concerns, choosing to be accommodating in order to get the project done.

Accommodation was the only one style that would work with him, since any effort I made to work out a compromise only triggered his suspicions and fears about being taken advantage of in a field he didn't know or trust. And collaboration was out of the question because his emotions were so close to the surface that it was unrealistic to sit down and try to negotiate anything. Thus, for all practical purposes, accommodation was the only alternative, except for walking away from the situation entirely. Because I placed a greater priority on completing the project than avoiding it, I chose accommodation over avoidance.

You may often find that your choice with a difficult person is between those two alternatives—avoidance and accommodation. A difficult person tends to use his difficult behavior to get his way. The Steamroller steamrolls, the Complainer complains, the Exploder explodes, and so forth, because they expect others to go meekly along with what they want to avoid the conflict. If the issues involved in the conflict aren't that important to you, it may be worth it to walk away or to give in. At least that way you preserve the peace or continue to work together on the other person's terms.

On the other hand, if you are willing to take some time and the issue is important enough to you, you might be able to use some other strategies to get more of what you want—most notably through compromise or collaboration. But then you need to consider the special needs making this person difficult to be able to work out a compromise or collaboration arrangement that addresses those needs.

For example, suppose you work in an office where one of your co-workers is constantly finding reasons to put you down. She criticizes your work to others, tells the boss you didn't do things you did, and you even suspect her of misdirecting your memos and mail, though you can't prove this and are afraid to lodge any accusations. You might be tempted to avoid this person or back down in meetings to avoid an open war, which might poison the atmosphere even more. However, if you take some time to dig beneath the surface, you might be able to uncover what is really wrong and find some peaceful compromise or collaborative solution. You might even turn this difficult person into an ally, or a friend.

Perhaps this person is acting in a hostile way towards you because she is jealous; if so, deal with the jealousy. If you remind her of someone who has hurt her in the past, deal with that. One way to reach these underlying problems is to find some time to talk about them. If the person seems resistant to talking to you, you might start with some small gestures to provide the basis for peace—go out of your way to say a friendly hello, offer some tickets at the office and include this person in your offer, and so on. In short, try to diffuse the person's underlying reasons for being difficult by being supportive, empathetic, and friendly to encourage the person to be pleasant to you in return.

Sure, you may feel motivated to avoid or squash a person who has been so difficult. That's the effect difficult people have. But if you fight against any such initial tendencies, you may be able to get to the root of the problem. Then, having cleared the air and undercut the person's reason for being difficult, you can proceed to find a resolution satisfying for you both.

Dealing with Common Types of Difficult People

While the general principles of conflict resolution still apply, certain strategies may be particularly helpful with certain types of difficult people. Following are a sample of these, though any difficult person may have a combination of traits (for example, a person who explodes may be a silent Clam at times). The key is to remain flexible, and adapt your approach to the particular person, his or her underlying needs, and your priorities in resolving or walking away from the situation.

The Steamroller/Sherman Tank Types

These are people who come on like gangbusters, thinking that if they push others around they will get their way, since others will back down.

Also, while some act like this because they are convinced they are right and are determined to show this to others, some fear they might be shown up for being wrong—a scary prospect, for it may undermine the Steamroller's image of him- or herself.

If the issue's not particularly important to you, your best bet is probably to avoid or accommodate. Give the Steamroller a wide berth, or give in to small things to calm him or her down. If you choose another tack, it's a good idea to begin by letting the person let off steam. Then, calmly and surely present your point of view, but avoid making the person feel wrong, since this is likely to inspire another round of hostile responses. Picture your role as that of a peacemaker who is above the fray. Meet the person's fury with your own inner serenity and calm. This will help the Steamroller put aside his or her aggression, and you can work things out from there.

The Undercover Attacker/Sniper Type

This is the secret saboteur who tries to bring others down with behind-the-stage machinations, cutting remarks, and other veiled shows of aggression. He or she commonly thinks this behavior is fully justified on the grounds that someone has done something wrong, and he or she is a secret avenger setting things right. Why secret? Because this Undercover Attacker/Sniper prefers to act behind the scenes, since he or she doesn't feel powerful enough to act openly. A battle with this type of person is like fighting with a guerrilla soldier.

If you decide that avoidance or learning to live with these attacks is not for you, the best way to deal with this Attacker/Sniper is first to bring the attack to the surface, then get to the underlying reasons. Let the Attacker know you are onto him by saying something like: "Was that meant as a put-down?" If the Undercover Attacker/Sniper tries to deny it, present your evidence. But keep your cool as you do this, so the Attacker doesn't feel *you* are attacking aggressively, which might only lead to an open battle.

As you continue to identify intended undercover attacks, the Undercover Attacker will finally realize you have recognized what he is doing; you have blown his cover. He'll realize he must now either stop the attacks or openly justify them. And once the attacks are brought to the surface, you can try to find out what's really bothering the Sniper/Attacker and find a way to deal with the problem.

The Angry Child/Exploder

This type doesn't just get angry; he or she gets furious and explodes like a child having a tantrum. Commonly, the person who does this feels very fearful and frustrated, and this is his or her way of gaining control. For example, a husband may erupt when he feels insanely jealous about something he thinks his wife is doing and he fears losing her or losing control, or an employer may blow up to get an unruly staff member back into line.

If you are on the receiving end of such a tirade, to avoid escalating things further (unless you decide to walk away from all this) let the Angry Child/Exploder finish yelling and screaming until she has finished venting. Or reassure the Angry Child/Exploder that you are listening and are ready to be responsive to calm her. The idea is to help the person feel she is still in control, while calming her down.

Then, when the person is calm again, just act as if she were an ordinary, reasonable person, as if the tantrum incident never happened. Politely and calmly offer to talk about the problem. You may find the Angry Child/Exploder is embarrassed and apologetic about the yelling and screaming incident. If so, accept any apologies to help her feel better. Otherwise it's probably best to shift the focus away from the incident, since the Angry Child/Exploder is likely to be eager to forget it happened. Once back in control, she would like to be seen as a responsible, rational adult.

The Complainer

There are two types of complainers: the Realistic Complainer and the Paranoid Complainer. While the Realistic Complainer is griping about real issues or events, the Paranoid Complainer is complaining about imaginary slights. In either case, however, the Complainer is griping about something and blaming others—either specific identifiable people or the world, generally—for all manner of wrongs. Sometimes, the Complainer may simply unload on you as a willing ear. But at other times, you may be at the brunt of the Complainer's attacks, berated for something you did or something he blames you for doing.

If the Complainer is talking about someone else, a common reaction is to tune him or her out. Alternatively, you may feel drawn to argue back in order to point out that what the Complainer is saying is untrue or unhelpful. But neither approach will really solve the basic problem. In the first case, the Complainer will have one more topic to talk about: you and your failure to listen. In the second case, the Complainer is likely just to get defensive, because you're attacking and haven't really responded to his or her complaints.

Instead, the key to dealing with the Complainer is listening at first. It doesn't matter whether the complaints are true or unfounded. The Complainer wants desperately to be heard. That's why he is constantly complaining—because he thinks no one is listening, taking him seriously, or doing what he says. His complaints usually arise out of frustration and a sense of being powerless. By listening, you help to give the person a feeling of power and an opportunity to discharge his frustration.

You should acknowledge or validate the Complainer by showing you have understood what he is saying, perhaps by repeating in other words a capsule description of what he has said. Then, once the Complainer has poured out his basic complaint, seek some closure. You might even imagine yourself a small claims judge hearing a petitioner present a case. If the person starts to repeat himself, as Complainers often do, you can calmly and respectfully interrupt to stop him from running on and on. Instead, try to shift the Complainer into a problem-solving mode. Ask questions: What does he want to *do* about the problem? Are there others who might help solve the problem? If he is blaming you for something, what can you do now to find some resolution? In short, acknowledge the Complainer's complaint, then move on.

Incidentally, in acknowledging the complaint, you don't have to agree with it. If it's true, certainly agree. If not, just point out that you understand and remain neutral. Emphasize that now that the complaint is clear, the question is what to do about it. You may have to shift the conversation back to the process of solving the problem more than once. But if you can break the pattern of complaining again and again, you can deal with the conflict by discussing it and thinking about realistic solutions. Or if the Complainer is mistaken in his complaints, help him see the mistake once he feels understood. Of course, if the Complainer keeps complaining and you feel you are going around in circles, you can always give up. But at least you will have given it a shot.

The Quiet Clams and Silent Types

These quiet types can be quiet for any number of reasons, and what's especially frustrating about dealing with them is that you don't know what the reason is. As a result, the key to resolving a conflict, unless you want to avoid the issue entirely, is to get the Clam or Silent Type to open up. You might have some suspicions (such as that he or she is angry about some incident but doesn't want to tell you), but it's not a good idea to act on that premise. If you are wrong, you can end up further escalating the conflict.

To get things out in the open, you might ask some open-ended questions, inviting more than a yes, no, or nod. If you get a brief reply, ask some follow-up questions, such as: "What's your feeling about that?" or "What happened that led you to feel that way?" Also, if you have any suspicions about what is wrong, and the person doesn't volunteer the information, you might share your suspicions to see if they are correct. For example, you might say, "I thought you might be avoiding me because you felt I slighted you at the office party." Keep probing or encouraging the Clam to speak, and even acknowledge that it may be difficult for him to share his feelings. For example, you might continue with something like, "I know you may not like talking about this, but if we can get this situation out in the open, we can deal with it and try to resolve it."

Show that you are willing to be supportive and empathetic no matter what the Clam says. Frequently, Clams clam up because they don't want to hurt other people's feelings, have been taught not to share their feelings, want to avoid confrontations, feel their opinions aren't valued, or are generally shy. Thus, it's particularly important to validate, support, and affirm the Clam. Show that whatever he or she says, you won't get angry, put him down, or be hurt yourself. Rather, emphasize that you truly value what he or she says and want to hear it, even if you disagree or don't like what he or she says.

It's easy to become impatient with Clams and Silent Types, because it's so hard to get a response. But if the issue is worth it, stick with it. Eventually the Clam may open up, like a reluctant oyster finally giving up its pearl. When that time comes, provide positive reinforcement. Show you appreciate that the Clam is talking to you, whether or not you agree or like what he or she is saying. And if the Clam should pause in responding, give him or her plenty of time to reply, so you don't cut off the response. It can be tempting to start talking to fill up the silence, but then you take the Clam off the hook and reinforce the Clam remaining a Clam. Keep up the pressure, as if you were patiently nudg-

178 ÷ Applying Your Reason

ing a stuck object out of a hole. As you see progress, continue to acknowledge it, to encourage the Clam to open up even more.

At the same time, be sensitive as to how far you can go. If you see the Clam suddenly digging in to resist some more, give the problem a rest. In that case, just thank the Clam for whatever communication you have gained so far, back off, and if it seems productive, try to arrange a time to meet again. You may not be able to resolve everything in one shot, but if you've gotten an opening, it's a start. Later, you can continue your attempts to work out the problem from the point you've reached.

Super-Agreeables Who Don't Come Through

Super-Agreeables can seem quite nice, not difficult at all, because they go out of their way to be helpful and liked. But at times this niceness and cooperative spirit can be the problem: You count on a Super-Agreeable who agrees to do something, but then he or she doesn't perform. A co-worker agrees to take on some responsibility, but doesn't; a friend agrees to do something with you and finds some reason to cancel at the last minute.

Assuming you feel you otherwise have a worthwhile relationship, the key to resolving the conflict is to show that you really want the person to be truthful. Insist that you want to know what the person *really* thinks and only want the person to say he or she will do what he really can or will do. Emphasize that what bothers you is the person's lack of follow-through on what he or she does agree to do, not whether he or she doesn't want to agree to something. Stress that you want the person to tell the truth, no matter what, and show that you will support and approve of the person for doing so.

Typically, a person agrees to more than he should out of a fear of telling an unpleasant truth and not being liked. So you want to provide support to help the person be truthful. You may have to provide this reassurance several times, until the person really feels comfortable and protected in sharing the facts with you or in saying no.

Once you get the facts out or see what the Super-Agreeable really thinks, you can talk honestly about any problems between you, and the main problem will disappear. You'll know where the person stands and what he will do, and you won't feel the letdown from his lack of follow-through.

Naysayers and Perennial Pessimists

It can be very discouraging to be around these negative types, who think things are bound to go wrong and are constantly worrying about things or saying no. Optimally, you may prefer to avoid such people, because they bring you down with them. If you can't, try to uncover the person's underlying fear that leads to the negativity in a particular situation. At the same time, don't let yourself get sucked into seeing the world from the Naysayer's point of view. Maintain your own optimism.

In dealing with the person's fear, keep in mind that Pessimists frequently feel a lack of control. They feel things—usually bad things—will just happen to them. Psychologists sometimes refer to this syndrome as a condition of "learned helplessness," as the person has a "locus of control" outside himself and sees himself as a victim or pawn in the hands of outside forces. Thus, help the person feel more in control by showing him the ways he can change what he doesn't like or prevent things from going wrong.

For example, if the person is coming up with reasons as why something won't work, try listening quietly for a while to acknowledge the person's concerns and show you understand. Then show that there is another point of view by describing realistic alternatives. If you can, use examples of past successes under similar circumstances or at least offer your optimistic view that something still can be done. You might say something like: "Let's at least try this new approach. We haven't tried it yet, and if we give it a chance, it may work."

Frequently, these negative types may also try to "yes, but" you. Whatever you propose, they come up with a reason why your suggestion won't work. Initially, try to answer with some hopeful alternatives. But if you see the "yes, but" pattern emerging, call the negative person on it. Point out that every time you suggest anything, he or she comes up with a reason why it won't work and you wonder if the person is open to *any* alternatives. Confronted by this honesty, the Naysayer may well back down.

On the other hand, if you see that the Naysayer or Pessimist is strongly invested in his position that things won't work, it may be better not to argue. You may find it hard to talk him out of his conviction, particularly when you aren't sure if the alternatives you are suggesting will work or not, and he *is* certain that it won't. In some cases, some gentle cajoling might be a way to do an end run around the negative person's conviction by suggesting that maybe it might be worth trying your ideas anyway as an experiment to see if they do work or provide at least a partial solution, or if not maybe they'll prove the negative person is right.

Alternatively, without confronting the negative person, you might try to come up with evidence that will lead him to recognize his pessimistic error independently or perhaps counter his underlying fear.

As you engage in these attempts to break through the Naysayer or Pessimist's negative shield, monitor your own reactions. Dealing with negative people can be very draining. They sap your energy and threaten to pull you into their negative perspective. If this starts happening, gently pull yourself away from the attempt to resolve the conflict or ask for a breather. It may be that you just cannot resolve the problem, though you did give it your best shot.

On the other hand, if you do see some movement in the person's attitude, it may be worth continuing to work towards a resolution or perhaps take a brief break and return. You may not be able to change the negative person's overall way of looking at the world, but at least you may be able to shift his way of looking at a particular situation. And that's all the change you need.

The Indecisives and Stallers

People who can't make a decision or keep putting one off are often afraid of results, unwilling to take responsibility for the outcome, scared that any decision will hurt someone, or find it hard to say no or yes. So they keep putting things off, feeling safer that way. This behavior can be very frustrating, especially if you're in a situation where your action awaits the other person's decision (for example, you cannot make reservations for your European vacation until your spouse decides whether he or she prefers to go in May or October). If you aren't already in conflict about the action in question, the indecision and stalling can lead to a conflict.

One approach is to take a more forceful position yourself (i.e., the competitive/confrontational approach to conflict) and assert the decision you want if you have the power to do so—though you must be diplomatic when you do this. Let the Indecisive feel comfortable with your control, or even feel as if he or she contributed to the process. The Indecisive is likely to go along with a good proposal and may be relieved the decision has been taken care of. The danger is that the Indecisive may go along with the decision to keep the peace, but retain misgivings. This could set the stage for more conflict later over the outcome.

If you really do want or need the Indecisive's decision, try to find out why he or she is hesitating, so you can get rid of this block. In doing so, you may have to be supportive and diplomatic, since the Indecisive may not be open with that information. Sometimes he or she is trying to avoid hurt feelings by stalling. And sometimes the Indecisive doesn't know the reason, but just has some vague unconscious fear about deciding. One key to getting the Indecisive to talk is to show you are supportive and won't be hurt by whatever he or she decides. You just want to know what the person really thinks, whatever that is. Once you have brought to the surface what's really going on for the Indecisive, you'll have a more solid basis for trying to resolve problems or make joint decisions. You will no longer be in the dark, battling a hidden reason that is causing the person to hold back.

Crazymakers

Crazymakers can be particularly unnerving. They bend and break the rules of ordinary human behavior, which are rooted in expectation and trust. You don't know what to expect; you don't trust what they will do. You can end up feeling that you are slipping and sliding in a sea of mud.

When you can't avoid dealing with a person who is behaving this way, a first step is to recognize this is happening. Don't get sucked into this person's view of the world or a particular situation. You will just internalize the contradictory or impossible expectations and feel crazy yourself. Rather, use your own awareness to help the other person see those contradictions. Then, try to find out what underlying factors are causing the person to act or think like this.

For example, suppose a person has repeatedly set up meetings with you, but has cancelled each one at the last minute and you're beginning to wonder if the person really wants this meeting. Rather than accepting the Crazymaker's bland apologies and setting up another meeting, you might ask the person point blank if there's some reason he or she doesn't want to meet with you now, and if so, if you can talk about that.

When you do point out contradictions and try to talk about the underlying reasons, wait for an interlude when things are calm, so you can raise these points diplomatically. For example, if someone is yelling at you for not having met his impossible expectations, this might not be the best time to confront him with the problem. You are likely to make him defensive or even angrier, because he may feel accused. Instead, aim for a time between incidents when you can broach the topic, or perhaps try to do so when the person first approaches you with impossible expectations. At that time, describe the problem in a calm and neutral way, so you appeal to the person's reason and encourage his or her involvement in finding a solution.

For example, you might say something like: "I'd really like to do _____ [you fill in the goal], but there are some obstacles to doing this, such as _____ and _____ [you fill in the obstacles]. This is what I see as the problem: _____ [you describe the contradictions]. So I hope we can work together to try to resolve this. Maybe we could _____ [suggest your proposal]."

Crazymaking is harder to deal with when it occurs in a close personal relationship between parents and children, spouses, and lovers, since the process is more subtle and more tied in with underlying needs. An example is the perfectionist parent who sets impossibly high standards for her child. When the child ultimately fails, the parent makes the mistake of blaming the child. In such relationships, passions and stakes can be much higher. However, where it's possible to deal with these situations without calling in some professional help, the basic principles are the same. Start by recognizing the conflicted expectations that lie at the root of the crazymaking. Once these are clear, try to distance yourself emotionally from the situation, so you feel calm and neutral and don't take the other person's point of view. Once in this calm and neutral state, find a time when you can point out the contradictions, if you can, to the Crazymaker. If he or she is willing to acknowledge and accept these, you can go on to the final stage—working out a mutually productive solution together.

And what if you can't solve the problem? What if the other person isn't willing to listen or work things out? What if your attempts to resolve things only make the person angrier and angrier? It may be that you can't do anything, and your only alternative is avoidance (avoid the person, end the relationship, quit the job) or continuing to suffer in silence, knowing the Crazymaker will give contradictory instructions or let you down again, if you feel that preserving the relationship or job is worth the price.

Being aware of the problem may not end the crazymaking, but it will let you set your priorities and choose your course of action. It will also help you feel secure in your own sanity and competence in the face of impossible demands.

Dealing with Other Difficult Types

What about the Perfectionists, Secret Forts, Innocent Liars, Resentful Altruists, Game Players, and other difficult types? As in many of the situations already described, the key is to get the problem behavior out on the table. On your own or together, try to identify the underlying reasons or needs causing the behavior.

Once you have clear reasons or needs in sight, you'll have a better idea of how to meet them so you can overcome the problem behavior and deal with any further conflicts without that problem standing in the way.

Specifically, find out why the Perfectionist is so demanding and point out why this behavior isn't necessary or is counterproductive. Let the Secret Fort know you want to know what's really wrong, because you sense he or she is bothered by something. Tell the Secret Liar that you feel he may not be completely candid with you (though don't call him a ''liar,'' which is apt to only provoke anger or further lies) and explain with empathy that you really need to know what the person thinks. Encourage the Resentful Altruist to express her true feelings. And call the Game Players on their games—though again, the key is diplomacy. Let them know you know what they're doing, but do it in a nice friendly tone, so they don't get mad. You might tell the ''yes, but-er'': ''Well, it sounds like every time I make a suggestion, you find a reason why it won't work. Do you really want to solve this problem? If so, maybe we can look for some other alternatives. But if not, maybe we should talk about something else.''

In Summary

When you encounter a difficult person, use a strategy tailored to that person's particular behavior problem. This strategy will vary from type to type, but use these key points as your guide:

- Become aware that the person is being difficult and note the type of difficult behavior he or she is exhibiting.

- Distance yourself from this behavior or the difficult person's point of view so you don't get sucked into his or her orientation. Stay calm and neutral.

- If you decide not to avoid the situation entirely, try to talk to the person and find out the underlying reasons for being difficult.

- Try to find a way of satisfying those underlying reasons or needs.

- Use mutual problem solving to resolve any other conflicts that become clear once the person's difficult behavior has been identified and is eliminated or controlled.

Section
Four

Using Your Intuition to Discover New Possibilities

Coming Up with Alternatives and Solutions

Once you've defined your problem, and are willing to work it through and consider alternative solutions, how do you find those alternatives? This chapter can help you by describing two key methods: brainstorming and looking within. You can brainstorm alone or with others, following a few rules to freely generate ideas. When you look within, you ask your inner expert for suggestions. Both methods help you maximize your creativity and apply it to finding a resolution by giving you a long list of alternative solutions to choose from. These methods can also be used to confirm—or reject—ideas you already have.

Brainstorming

Brainstorming has gone mainstream, and is used by many groups and organizations to come up with ideas for everything from throwing a party to reorganizing a company. It can likewise be used to come up with new ideas for resolving a conflict, and besides the commonly used methods of group brainstorming, you can use some other techniques described in this chapter to generate ideas, and adapt the process to your own preferred style. Not everyone, for example, is at their best in brainstorming by calling out ideas in a group.

When you brainstorm, you try to come up with as many possible solutions as you can without trying to decide what is appropriate. By not trying to edit or control your thoughts, you unleash your creativity. Then, the second stage is to think realistically about your ideas and decide which to implement. But in the first stage, let your intuitive part come up with ideas as quickly as it can. Wait until later for the editor to come in to choose and select.

Creative artists and inventors use this process to develop their ideas, and that's what I do too when I write, design games, or come up with new business ideas. In the first phase, I simply sit down at the computer or drawing board without saying, "This has to be perfect." In the second phase, I do the editing or selecting.

The reason not to do any selection or editing in the first stage is that this can block the process. If you think something should be a certain way in advance, you'll inhibit your creativity because the creative part of yourself gets the idea that it has to come up with a fully finished, realized concept. Thus, a barrier of fear goes up, and the creative flow shuts down.

It's the same in dealing with conflicts, with other people or within yourself. Any particular conflict can be resolved in many different ways. But sometimes people get stuck because they look for the one perfect resolution and feel there are only certain ways of achieving it. Popular advice columns such as "Dear Abby" perpetuate this notion. They propose the "right" solution. The truth is that if you describe the same situation to several other people, you will often find just as many proposed solutions—and many of them will be excellent.

So open your mind to possibilities, since there is no set way of dealing with any conflict. People have different ways of approaching each problem, depending on personalities, interests, circumstances, and many other factors. Let yourself go in brainstorming to tap into all the possibilities your creative mind can generate. In the editing phase of the process, you can select the approach or approaches you feel are most appropriate for resolving the conflict.

Brainstorming on Your Own

If you are brainstorming on your own, a good way to come up with ideas is to take a sheet of paper or a notebook and set aside ten or fifteen minutes for stage one. In a quiet place free of distractions, focus on the problem; as quickly as possible, think of as many ideas as you can for solving it. You might even imagine that someone else has come to you with this problem and you are giving this person advice to help you feel more detached and objective towards the problem.

As the ideas come to you, write them down. Write quickly so you don't lose your train of thought. Don't give yourself time to think about whether the ideas are silly or impractical. You don't want to edit or censor them in any way. You can choose the good ones later.

If the ideas don't come at first, keep concentrating for the time period you have set. You'll find that focusing your attention will help to get the ideas started; then one idea can start the flow of more. Also, consider adding onto or modifying your ideas to come up with even more possibilities, or think about opposites or variations on a theme (such as, besides talking to that person, bring a third party in to help you talk to that person). For example, you might write down your thoughts about different ways to resolve a conflict with someone, besides the more obvious one of talking to someone about the problem. When you think of corollaries, don't think of them as substitutes to be used *instead of* the original. Consider them as *additional* ideas to add to your brainstorming list, since you want to include as many ideas as possible.

It's unlikely that you will have no ideas. If you are slowing down, stop at the end of the time limit. But if you are still getting all sorts of ideas, keep going as long as they are flowing freely.

When you feel sure you have finished generating ideas, go over them. Rate them from 1 (very good) to 5 (not very good at all); give the idea a 3 if you feel neutral or aren't sure yet. Afterwards, you can take the ideas you rated the most highly and put them into practice.

If you need further clarification on how to apply a particular idea, you can go through the brainstorming process again, focusing on ways to make the idea work.

If you find brainstorming on your own too difficult, that may be because it's hard to get the distance and freedom to be creative when you're in the midst of a problem. If you are feeling stuck, try brainstorming with another person or in a small group for a fresh perspective on your problem.

Brainstorming with Others

Sometimes brainstorming with others is just what you need to get unstuck when you have exhausted your own ideas on what to do. To brainstorm with others, you might get together with a friend or associate or form a small group of six to eight people. You might even draft some dinner guests into a quick brainstorming session. If the others would like to brainstorm for solutions to their own problems, you might take turns doing this in whatever type of brainstorming group you have put together.

To begin the brainstorming process, you (or whoever's problem is being brainstormed) should have a sheet of paper and a pencil to record any ideas. Or use a large board that everyone can see. With four or more people, sit in a circle or around a table, so everyone can face each other and each person's contribution will take on equal value. When you write down ideas, don't write down the names of whoever has made that suggestion. Besides being faster, this frees everyone to be free and spontaneous.

To kick off the brainstorming, describe your conflict situation. Preferably use the first person, if you feel comfortable doing this. Or if this makes you uncomfortable, describe the situation in the third person, as if it happened to someone else. Make your description as neutral as possible as you present the facts of what occurred, so you give everyone an objective picture of the situation. Don't advance any preconceptions about what you think the solution should be. Describe your perspective, and then the other party's perspective.

After you describe the situation, allow anyone to ask questions to clarify what the problem is before the problem solving begins. Keep the questioning to factual, clarifying questions. Don't get sucked into subjective or accusing questions, such as "Why didn't you _____?" or "Were you aware of that person's feelings about _____?"

Once everyone has a clear understanding of the conflict, go on to the problem-solving stage. You can do this in one of three ways:

1. Let everyone brainstorm individually and out loud at first, while you write down ideas and say nothing. (You can then do some on-the-spot brainstorming yourself to contribute your ideas when the others are finished.)

2. You start brainstorming your own ideas aloud and write down these

ideas while others listen. (You'll let others brainstorm afterwards, while you just listen and write.)

3. You and everyone else all brainstorm at the same time, and you write down any ideas that come up as before.

Try experimenting with these different methods to find out which is most comfortable and productive for you.

Whichever approach you use, whoever is brainstorming should throw out as many suggestions as possible. Don't go in any particular order. Everyone should contribute ideas as they think of them. Feel free to piggyback or expand on an idea you have heard; but don't criticize or put down other ideas, because that can interfere with the creativity flow by making others feel self-conscious. Avoid being judgmental, so others won't be afraid to make suggestions. The secret to successful brainstorming is that everything is possible, and nothing should be judged wrong, ridiculous, or unworkable in advance.

By the same token, if you are listening as other people come up with ideas for you, don't make comments about why it won't work or how you've tried it before. That means no "yes, but" or "but I tried that" comments—such comments will interrupt the creative flow. Simply write down whatever people say. You can eliminate the unworkable or previously tried ideas later.

In writing down these comments, write down just enough to trigger your memory. You don't have to write everything down. Record as much as you can at the time, so you don't slow down the process when you take notes.

Once the first stage of brainstorming is over, go through the list of ideas you have recorded and choose what makes the most sense to you as solutions to the conflict. To do so, use a ranking system from 1 to 5. Put a 1 next to things you most want to do, a 2 next to what you'd like to do if possible, 3 next to the maybes, 4 for the probably-nots, and 5 for the definite nos. Afterwards, you can put the more practical and highest priority solution or solutions into practice right away.

Examples of Brainstorming

Here are some representative examples from a workshop to show how the process works. People came in with their problems, brainstormed as a small group, and all of them came away with new ideas they could use to resolve their conflicts.

One woman was very concerned about getting a new "dream" job, which was a perfect match for her skills. But she was scared, because the job was in a new field and she would have to leave her old career. She explained that she had been taking steps to make the change, such as writing up a resume, but she felt blocked by her fear. She was undergoing a real inner conflict. While she was planning to apply for the job, she was afraid of putting out a lot of energy and not being chosen. "I may not try as hard as I should or could to really get it," she concluded.

In response, the two men she was brainstorming with had all sorts of suggestions, and she just listened, since she felt stuck in coming up with new ideas herself. Some of the possibilities included:

- Apply for the job; forget about your fear, and apply just for the adventure of it.

- Think of how well you will do in the job when you get it.

- Don't think of this as the only great job opportunity you will get; recognize that there will be many others.

- Think about the other situations you have been in where you have been afraid and things worked out; realize that you will survive this one, too.

- Visualize yourself getting the job: See your employer hiring you enthusiastically, on the spot.

- Think of all the good qualities you have which make you very employable; you'll have more confidence when you interview and will be more likely to get the job.

- Think of this job interview as one more step in the learning process; even if you don't get this job, your effort isn't wasted. You'll have prepared yourself, so you'll be ready for the next job that comes along.

As you can see from this example, brainstorming can be as helpful in dealing with feelings as it can be in coming up with concrete action plans.

Another woman confessed to hating her teaching job, which she felt she had to stick with for another eight months, since the school term had just started. After a brainstorming session, she too came away with a long list of useful ideas. As she described the problem, she had trouble getting along with the other people at work. She felt like she was working in a prison and felt out of sync with the school's philosophy and policies. As she put it:

I only took the job because I wanted to make enough money to go over-seas. But I don't like teaching. How can I avoid having conflicts with peo-ple and being critical of where I'm working, since I so hate the job? . . . The school feels like a prison . . . but I have to control my feelings. My real problem is how to stay nice on a job that I hate.

Some of the suggestions she got were serious; others were humor-ous, outrageous things she could do to get even or show what she really thought of the system. But even if all the ideas weren't practical, they helped her feel better about where she was working and enabled her to release some of the anger and tension she felt. So even if she couldn't carry them out, she felt better just thinking about them as possibilities. It was a symbolic release, one she felt she couldn't get in reality. At the same time, once others started throwing out suggestions, this helped her become unstuck in thinking of things she might do. She soon had plenty of her own ideas to add to the list, as well.

Just to get a flavor of the suggestions she received, here is a sampling:

- Don't talk to the other teachers.
- Eat in the park.
- Stay away from the other teachers.
- Keep your own future goal constantly in mind; the more hope you have about the future, the better you can put up with the way things are now.
- Pamper yourself to compensate for what you are suffering now; take bubble baths, or treat yourself to weekly trips to the movies.
- Try to find fulfilling things to do when you are off the job.
- If you find another teacher who seems a little sympathetic, tell him or her what you really think.
- Find a support group of like people who are also in transition and hate their jobs.
- Form a support group for recovering teachers.
- Throw dishes so you feel better.
- Take a picture of the worst person on your job and put that picture on a punching bag, paint circles on it, and throw darts at it.
- Be as playful as you can to have fun with the kids.
- Create a dramatic play about your situation, and have your kids put it on as their class play.

- If there's one teacher you can talk to, whisper quietly: "We can break out of here soon. Pass it on."
- Write the principal's name on dozens of subscription cards to all sorts of magazines and send them in.

In another case, a man I was consulting with (let's call him Joe), wasn't sure what to do about a partnership he was involved in. Joe had developed a new technology in a new field and felt his business partner, Steve, could help him make connections in that industry, as well as help him learn what to do in that industry. Then, the plan was for them to raise the money from investors to fund his invention. And initially, he thought things were going well, because his partner did open some doors for him and introduce him to people who might want to work on the project.

However, after about a month, as he began to learn about the industry himself, he found that Steve often seemed overly brash and even off-putting. Also, his partner had some disagreements with some people who expressed interest in working on the project and helping them raise funds. He began to wonder if Steve might be a liability and if he should get out of the agreement while it was still early enough to do so. Joe said to me, "I just don't know if I can trust him. Yet, he also seems really enthusiastic and has put a lot of effort into this. And he is still contacting people, so maybe he might still be able to get in the funding."

At my suggestion, he began brainstorming different possibilities that he could assess later to decide which option to choose. He came up with a number of viable options. He could:

- Have a conversation with his partner to express his concerns; maybe Steve will be able to explain some of the things that have bothered him or might change his behavior.
- Offer to do some of the fundraising himself, once Steve has made the introductions.
- Write down more specifically what his partner does that bothers him; this way he can be more specific in talking to Steve—and if things don't work out, he would have documented the problem areas and provided himself with good cause for terminating the partnership.
- Hang onto his current partnership until he has assessed other possibilities; he might put out some cautious feelers to see if anyone

else is interested in going into a partnership with him on the invention.

- Talk to a lawyer about his concerns and get legal advice on what to do.

- Talk to a trusted friend and get feedback on the situation.

- Set up a few meetings to introduce his invention to potential investors and take a more active role in presenting his invention to others.

- Wait for another week or two before he did anything and see if the benefits of Steve's behavior (contacting investors and opening doors for Joe) outweigh the negatives (his abrasive manner that turns some people off) or vice versa. Meanwhile, Joe will document what happens in a diary, just in case he needs the record for later.

Outcomes of Brainstorming

The advantage of using this brainstorming process, particularly in a group, is that it can bring new thinking to a stalemated situation. As one person in the group observed:

It was like there was a new spark of energy in dealing with this old problem. I might have thought about some of these ideas before, but I didn't do anything with them. The brainstorming provided another way of hearing these ideas said, and that helped to clear up the fog I had experienced about this situation. Now I feel like I can move ahead.

Not all of the proposed solutions may be workable. Some may be offered purely for their humor or to show how creative people can be in coming up with unique, even far-out ideas. But generally, you can expect that at least some of the ideas will be useful. In the workshop, all the participants felt they had discovered some new solutions they could put to use.

Sometimes, too, as the participants discovered, just engaging in the process with helpful, supportive people helped them rethink old ideas in a new, "this can work" light.

One man in the workshop had this experience. His friend's wife had come down with Parkinson's disease and had been an invalid for four years, and would only continue to deteriorate as the disease progressed. The friend had been struggling with the question of whether he should stay with her during her illness. He was feeling more and more depressed by the situation, but he felt trapped by his guilt. As the man in the workshop explained:

> *After four years, the situation has become overwhelming for him. He comes home from work and realizes his wife isn't getting any better. Somebody has to take care of her while he's at work. He's not having his own needs met, but he's hesitant to find out what would be good for him.*
>
> *I had some ideas about what he should do, such as getting a support network of friends or going to support groups for others in this situation. Or he might get friends and neighbors to help with the shopping. Or maybe he should look at his needs in the relationship, and if he felt he couldn't get them satisfied, find a way to break away. But I felt afraid to tell him anything. I didn't know what to say.*

However, when the people in his brainstorming group said to do exactly the things he had been thinking, he felt supported. He had been hesitant to tell his friend what he really thought, because he thought it might seem he was urging his friend to be irresponsible. After all, pulling away from this depressing situation meant pulling away entirely or to some degree from an ill and needy woman. Yet, the man felt that was what his friend both needed to do and wanted to do to preserve his own sanity and health. He also felt the friend needed support, both with "what to do" ideas and emotional concern to help him make the break as easy as possible for the woman.

Hearing these ideas echoed by the group helped give him the push he needed. "Now I feel I'm ready to tell my friend what I really think," he said at the end of the session. "Then, my friend can decide to do what he wants. And I think my support will help him do what he really needs to do. I was experiencing a lot of emotional turmoil about deciding how to handle this situation, but now I feel that is over, because I know what to do."

Enhancing the Power of Brainstorming in Your Life

To make the brainstorming process even more useful to you in the future, work with it on a regular basis whether to resolve everyday conflicts or develop creative ideas. Consider it regular exercise that will help keep the creative, intuitive part of your mind well-tuned for producing ideas. It's like keeping a car engine lubricated and turning on the motor regularly, so it is ready to go when you need it. Ten to fifteen minutes a day might be good to keep your intuition tuned. And if you have no conflict in your life to work on, think of another topic to brainstorm about and let your mind go.

Another way to use brainstorming is to get together with friends or contacts at work to get their help in resolving a particular problem or to practice brainstorming generally. All sorts of support groups and interest groups deal with particular topics. Why not put together a brainstorming group?

Looking Within

Another way to tap into your intuitive, creative ability to resolve conflicts is to employ what we call the Inner Expert process. In this process, instead of coming up with as many ideas as possible in a short time, you call on your inner self from a relaxed, altered state of consciousness. The techniques of relaxation and visualization should be familiar if you have already used them to release conflict, reduce anger, or determine which conflict-handling style to use in a particular situation. Once again, these techniques can give you answers hidden to your everyday, conscious mind.

In using this process, you first get relaxed using any number of methods. Then, you go within yourself in a mild trancelike state (which is like a mild hypnosis or meditation), where you are focused yet relaxed. You imagine your inner self to be an expert and you have a talk with this person.

You can carry on this dialogue with your inner expert in a number of ways. You can:

- See an expert appear on a TV or computer screen.
- Meet with somebody in a workshop.
- Call on a person you already know.
- Ask for advice from a teacher you have met.

In short, you can visualize anybody who looks helpful and knowledgeable, since in reality you are consulting a helpful, knowledgeable part of yourself.

Visualization

The following visualization is designed to help you relax and contact your inner expert. Eventually, as you work with this inner part of yourself more frequently, you will probably not need to go through the entire process. Instead, you can call on this inner expert almost automatically, just by getting into a relaxed state and asking your inner expert to appear. But initially, this somewhat lengthy visualization will help. Read it to yourself and use it as a general guide; put it on a tape and listen to it; ask a friend to read it to you while you get relaxed.

Start off by relaxing. Close your eyes and breathe deeply several times until you feel very comfortable and relaxed. If you know what question or conflict you want to ask about, let this appear in your mind. Or you can wait and ask the question later, if you are not sure now.

Just focus on your breathing going in and out, in and out, to get calm and relaxed. Feel yourself getting calm and relaxed and very comfortable, as you notice your breathing going in, and out, in, and out. Yet, even as you get relaxed, you'll be able to hear the sound of my voice and stay alert and awake.

Now imagine yourself in a special place where you feel very comfortable and very safe. It could be your room, a meadow, a place in the country where you like to go, wherever you want.

See yourself there now and observe what's around you. Maybe there are books around; maybe you see a computer screen; maybe you are in the country and see trees and grass. Wherever you are, feel yourself very much a part of the environment.

Then, as you look up, you notice somebody coming towards you. It might be somebody you have seen before, or it might be somebody totally new. Say hello to this person and know that this person is here to help you and has information to give you.

Invite the person to sit down with you, maybe on a chair, maybe on the grass, maybe on a cushion. Spend a little bit of time getting to know this person. Ask this person who he or she is. Ask what he or she does. And maybe tell the person a little bit about yourself.

As you talk about yourself, tell the person about conflict situation you are involved in. This conflict may be something you had in mind before you began this experience or something you are thinking about right now.

Describe the situation to this person, and notice that he or she is very sympathetic, understanding, and quietly listens as you talk. Maybe this person has a few questions to ask you so you can explain the situation in more detail. I'll be quiet for a few moments to give you a chance to explain the problem, so this person really understands what it is.

(Pause 15–30 seconds.)

Now that you've finished explaining the problem, this person has some answers and suggestions for you. Just listen as he or she tells you what to do.

These may be ideas you've never heard before or ideas you have thought of but aren't sure about. Just listen receptively. Don't try to judge or evaluate. Just listen as the ideas come to you.

(Pause 15–30 seconds.)

Now, ask if this person has any more suggestions. Or if there is something you haven't understood, ask this person to explain a little more. Again, just listen to the answers.

(Pause 10–15 seconds.)

Now if you have another question, ask it or if you are concerned about another conflict, you can ask about this, too.

This time, your teacher will show you something. You will ask your question, and to answer it, he or she will take you to another place where you will see a screen or a stage. That's where you will see your answer played out for you.

So ask your question now and follow your teacher or expert as he or she leads you. Then, in this place you will discover your answer, for you will see it appear in front of you. Maybe it will appear in words, like a headline. Or maybe you will see a drama play itself out in front of you on the stage or screen.

Just see what happens. And again, don't try to plan anything. Just receive.

(Pause 15–30 seconds.)

Now your teacher or expert is finishing the answer. If you have seen anything in front of you, it starts to fade or vanish. Now it's gone and your teacher or expert leads you back to where you started.

Thank your expert or teacher and start to say goodbye. As you do, know that you can always call on this teacher or expert whenever you want, whenever you have a question, problem, or conflict and you want some answers. You can ask a question and get an answer or you can have your expert take you and show you the answer, whichever you prefer.

So now you see your teacher or expert leaving, and you feel very complete. As you do, I'm going to start counting backwards from five to one, and as I do, you'll become more and more awake and alert and come back into the room. Five, four, more and more awake. Three, two, almost back. One. And you're back in the room.

Getting Your Answer

Your answer may come in any number of forms. Some people get it in the form of very practical, down-to-earth advice. Others get it in the form of images or pictures, which may need some interpretation. Some find their answer from a single expert; others have multiple experts come to them with advice. Following are examples of different ways you might get this help.

1. **Direct Advice.** One of the most common ways to expect an answer is in the form of direct advice. This happened to one woman who wanted to know if she was doing enough and making the proper progress in developing an arts career. As she described it, her answer came back thus:

> *I was going along a path when this woman came along, and she was very practical and no-nonsense about telling me what to do . . . I asked her if I was really doing enough and making the proper progress in the arts . . . So she said, "Don't worry about it. You're doing all you can. The main problem is that you worry too much. So don't worry."*

But was this good advice? The woman thought so, because as she explained: "I don't know what else I can do at this point to further my career. I'm making all the progress I can. This tells me I have to keep a balance between work and doing something that I like. That will help me stop worrying, like the expert said."

2. **Indirect or Symbolic Advice.** Should your answer come to you in the form of symbols or pictures, you have to interpret them, since there is no particular thing that individual symbols or pictures mean. What's significant is what those images mean to *you*. It is possible that some images will reflect common cultural meanings for that image, since you are influenced by general cultural trends as well as your own experience. For instance, you might see red roses as love or champagne as victory, because red roses are commonly given to a lover; champagne is commonly used to toast a win. What's important is what the images mean to you, rather than the one-size-fits-all interpretations provided in some of the dreams and symbols books. While some of those interpretations may fit some people, they are too simplistic; people have different experiences and cultural backgrounds that can affect the meanings of different images.

The following example illustrates the process of reviewing the images you saw to interpret their meanings or how they answer your question. In this case, Roberta, a woman at a workshop asked what to do about her fear of being more assertive in her job and relationships. As she reported:

> *After I asked about my problem, I used a visualization and found myself in a meadow, where I met a very wise old guide, an Indian or the spirit of*

an Indian. The guide lifted her hand in an upward movement, pointed
ahead, and I saw a big lake in front of her. Then, she moved forward
toward the water and it rippled, and I felt like it was releasing the fears.
Then her hand went up and I felt a sensation of power.

Later, Roberta discussed her visualization and what she thought it meant. She thought of the water as an image of cleansing and purification, a common association for water, and felt this image meant she should imagine cleansing herself of her fears; she would then feel more centered and wouldn't be blocked from acting by her fears. This realization gave her a feeling of empowerment to deal with a troubling situation in her life.

In addition, since Roberta had found an image that could help release her current fears, she could use this same image in the future to dispel other fears. As I explained at the workshop: "Since you associate the image of water with cleansing and releasing fears, you can return to that lake whenever you feel burdened by fear. Just dump whatever fear is bothering you into the lake and watch it float away or sink. Then, you can walk away from the lake feeling cleansed and released of your fear."

3. **Getting Your Answer in Feelings.** Sometimes you may get an answer in the form of a nonverbal sensation or feeling, which can give you a yes or no. An example is the experience of one man who was experiencing inner conflict because he wondered if he was going in the right direction in his life. Since he wasn't sure, he felt himself pulled in many directions. But then he experienced a sense of certainty about what to do next, after he imagined himself walking on a ridge. Though the guide he passed said nothing, he had a feeling that his guide was letting him know he was doing fine. As he explained:

I was on a deserted ridge, and initially I didn't see anyone else around.
But after a while, I saw this guru coming by, and I told him I had a question
dealing with directions and time. "I'm not sure what to do," I told him. "I
feel I've been moving ahead in my life, but I'm not sure if I'm moving in
the right direction."

Then, somehow, I got an answer. There was no dialogue. But I suddenly I
had a feeling that I'd been wanting to get away from things, and my job
was one more of those things I wanted to get rid of. But I also had a sud-

den feeling of security thinking about where I am now. I felt that I didn't want to go on to another job. I'd rather feel that security of staying put for a while.

Then, I felt what I really need to do is slow down for now, just relax, and the ideas will come. When I'm ready I'll know where to go next. But for now, the message—or more precisely, the feeling—was that I should stay where I am and enjoy it more. I shouldn't take things so seriously. I should allow more vitality into my life. Now I feel freer to keep doing what I'm doing, and once I'm finished with the job, I can move on.

4. **Getting Your Answer from Multiple Guides.** In some cases, more than one teacher or guide will appear with your message. If so, this can be a further reassurance that your message is a good one for you now. It's as if you have gotten confirming opinions from a number of doctors.

For instance, a man who wasn't sure what to do about improving his personal relationships found a group of teachers surrounding him with suggestions. They were all noted therapists, and since he worked as a psychologist, the appearance of many teachers from his own field was doubly reassuring. As he noted: "They told me I need to share more information about myself. They said I should express myself more and not worry so much."

Getting Confirmation of Previous Advice or Current Plans

This technique of working with a teacher or guide is also useful in confirming ideas you already have or suggestions from others about doing something. Your message can act as a go-ahead or reassure you about something you are thinking of doing but aren't sure whether to do or not. The message from a teacher or guide is like getting the stamp of approval, because your guides or inner self are telling you clearly that what you want to do or have considered is okay.

Of course, if you get a different message, this suggests you need to look at things differently. You might look more closely at the advice you have gotten from different sources to sift and weigh alternatives. You might try more visualizations to expand your previous ideas or come up with new ones. Whatever you do, trust your inner expert to point you towards what you feel is or isn't the appropriate thing to do in the circumstances.

Your Inner Expert Has Many Guises

When you get information from your inner expert, teacher, or guide, essentially you are objectifying or personifying your own self. Using visualization to "make contact" with your Inner Expert can make it easier to get that information from this "separate" inner self and enable you to have a conversation or simply be receptive to this inner wisdom. This wisdom from within can be particularly helpful in a conflict situation, because this inner voice or vision, however you perceive it, can give you guidance on what choice to make. Then, you can feel a greater sense of certainty and reassurance that you have made the right choice.

You may get this information in different ways, since different people have different ways of perceiving information. Some people are very visual and may see an image or picture of their expert. Other people may get this information verbally; they may not see anyone but may hear what their expert is saying as a voice. Still others may experience a sense of knowing or telepathic communication.

Thus, when you work with this technique of looking inward, notice that you get your information in different ways and notice which way feels more natural or comfortable for you. It doesn't matter which way you get your information—through pictures, sounds, or through your senses. All ways are equally valid, so when you work with this technique in the future, use whatever feels right. Select the approach that works best for you. While your Inner Expert may appear to you in various forms when you first start using these techniques, you may find you gain more help from certain Inner Experts or feel more rapport with them. If so, you can consciously call on those Inner Experts to help you in the future. The process is a little like meeting a lot of new friends who offer different types of help; you then choose among those who you prefer to become closer to and spend more time with in the future.

14

Turning Your Conflicts into Creative Opportunities

While having peace and harmony in relationships and within oneself are ideals, some conflicts are almost inevitable. When we relate to others, we encounter people with different goals, values, interests, and priorities. And individually, we can be torn by different choices and uncertainties about which of our different goals, values, interests, and priorities are most applicable in a particular situation. A key goal of using the conflict resolution techniques in this book is to resolve a conflict and restore harmony. At the same time, you can use conflict as a source of learning and personal growth in a number of ways, using your intuition to build on your knowledge about the situation to decide what to do.

First, you can draw on the conflict to gain insights about yourself. You might use a conflict as an indicator that it is time to make major changes in yourself, in a relationship, or in an organization. You might also learn from a conflict how better to deal with your feelings and react in future conflicts. And you might use a conflict to notice patterns of attitudes, interactions, or individual responses that contribute to conflicts, so you can work on changing these.

See What You Can Learn

Conflicts can be turned into excellent learning experiences if you take time later to look at what led up to the conflict and what happened during it. You can learn more about yourself, the others you are in conflict with, or the environmental setting contributing to the conflict. This knowledge might help you:

- Decide what to do in a conflict and avoid a future recurrence.

- Notice recurring patterns with the same people or the same issues, so you can examine how that pattern contributes to conflict and perhaps alter the pattern to reduce or eliminate the potential for conflict.

- Look into the causes of the recent conflict to discover if you need to make larger changes in your life, your actions, or the friends and associates you choose.

In some cases, the recurring patterns of conflict you identify may be due to habitual behavior patterns that are hard to break. But by becoming aware, you can start the process of breaking the habit.

For instance, that's what happened for Barbara, who realized that she was in a series of codependent relationships with men who had drinking problems. She had low feelings of self-esteem and found it made her feel better when she became involved with a man who needed her because of his own weakness. As the relationship continued, however, she would become angry at the man for being weak and not achieving the high goals she set for him.

Due to her frustration, she would start nagging the man to pull himself together and work harder, and he would fight back in return. The result was often huge yelling arguments, even physical battles, leading Barbara to find herself battered and bruised. Yet afterwards they would make up, and again Barbara would feel good because she felt her boyfriend still needed and loved her, until the next blowup. And so the pattern continued until hostility and confusion split the relationship apart. But then Barbara would be drawn to the same type of man, setting herself up for a similar pattern of crisis.

To break the pattern, Barbara needed to look at these conflicts and identify the pattern, so she could work on breaking the cycle. One way Barbara determined to do this is what many women in codependent relationships resolve: to avoid such men in the future. If they see a man has a certain type of character, they recognize this quality and pull away before getting involved. At first it was tough for Barbara to use this strategy, since her attraction to needy men was filling her needs.

But once she recognized the destructive pattern and fought against it, she was eventually able to pull away by finding other interests and building up her self-esteem. The relationship she ultimately allowed to develop was much healthier, more fulfilling, and much less conflict-ridden.

In other cases, conflict patterns may be more personalized, but can be changed, too, with some awareness and work. For instance, Philip, like Jim in Chapter 10, was dealing with a cooling male friendship, but unlike Jim, realized that he had a pattern of such relationships. Initially he would develop friendships with men he met at work or in social groups. After they got to know each other, they would open up and share their more personal concerns, such as their fears about jobs, their hopes for meeting women, their attitudes towards parents, and their future goals. But after a year or two, Philip realized, a certain coolness seemed to develop with these friends and eventually they would drift away from each other. He blamed himself for having done something to cause this.

Then, when Philip looked more closely at the situation, he came to a number of realizations about this and other past relationships. He realized that the growing coolness at the end of all these relationships was not because of anything he had done, so he needn't blame himself. Rather, these relationships experienced the normal kind of drifting away that occurs when people get involved in different activities and grow in different directions. Philip also came to realize that this drifting away might sometimes be due to personal issues confronting his friends and have nothing to do with him, so he shouldn't take what happened personally. Thus, by looking at past patterns, Philip came to realize it might be appropriate to relax, let the ending relationship go, and find another to fill this need for male companionship.

Likewise, you might find it helpful to look for patterns of conflict in past or current relationships to learn about the reasons for such a conflict. And even if a current conflict doesn't point to a recurring pattern, you can use it as an opportunity to learn something about yourself and make decisions about future actions and directions.

To gain these insights from a conflict, set aside some time to reflect on the problem. Think of all the ways you can learn and benefit from the current conflict, even though you may feel there is nothing good about the experience at the time. You may still be able to draw a silver lining out of the storm of conflict. This positive, solution-oriented approach might show you the problem isn't as bad as you think; and you might see new possibilities for change and growth.

Going Within Yourself After Conflict

A key to getting ideas on how to benefit from a conflict situation or any other bad experience is to look within and seek answers from your inner self. This will help you work through and process the experience, so you can learn from and resolve it in your mind. You'll feel more complete about whatever happened and ready to move on. I have written extensively about the value of this process of looking within for answers and guidance in several previous books: *Mind Power: Picture Your Way to Success in Business* (New York: iUniverse 2006; originally, Prentice Hall, 1987) and *The Empowered Mind: How to Harness the Creative Force Within You* (New York: iUniverse 2006; originally, Prentice Hall, 1994).

To help make the connection with your inner self, use visualization to get into an altered state of consciousness. You can also use automatic writing or recording to achieve this state; you start by relaxing with something nearby on which you can write or record your thoughts. Then, in this relaxed, spacey state, start writing or talking, just letting the thoughts flow out. Write down or say whatever comes, without trying to analyze or judge.

This automatic writing or talking will not only tap into your unconscious, but will provide a record of what you think or observe. However you reach this altered state, once there think of the conflict experience as a picture in a frame or video image on the screen. This way you can see what happened as separate from you, as if you are merely an observer, a moviegoer in a theater, or a reader looking through a magazine.

From this neutral, relaxed state, look at what happened as if it happened to someone else. You can then learn from it, examine what caused it, and imagine what you might do next as a result. Use your conscious, observing mind to ask questions you want to have answered, such as: "How can I learn from what happened?" "What caused it to occur?" "What can I do differently in the future to avoid this problem?"

After you ask your question, look at the picture or screen and wait receptively for answers to come in any form. You may see a visual image or scene played out in front of you; the words answering your question may appear; a voice may speak the answer to you. Different people have different ways of receiving information. Your answer may depend on whether your primary mode of reception is visual, auditory, or sensory. The important thing is to stay in this open, receptive state as you get your answers, so you can accept whatever comes. Later you can choose among these answers to determine what makes the most sense, much as in brainstorming for new ideas. For now, just listen, see, or feel whatever comes.

When you are finished getting these ideas, imagine the conflict or bad experience out of your life for good. You might use a physical gesture to sweep the bad experience out of your life or visualize such an action. For example, if you have been viewing a picture or a screen in your mind, you might see yourself tearing up the picture or see the screen shatter to bits or burn up. Such a visual image will help you believe the conflict is over and no longer part of your life.

Keeping Your Conflicts in Perspective

Sometimes the bad feelings generated can make the conflict loom much larger in your mind than it is and undermine your sense of direction or self-esteem. Such feelings can be a block to learning from conflict in addition to making you miserable.

For example, a woman having a noise dispute with her neighbors kept a notebook of each hostile encounter she had with them. As the list grew in size, so did the problem in her mind. Soon she wasn't only thinking about the conflict when embroiled in it but at other times during the day. She mulled over who did or said what, considered what to do next in response, and variously felt hostile, angry, or depressed every time she reviewed or anticipated a new blowup.

By contrast, you should look at any conflict as only a small portion of your life and remind yourself not to let it grow larger, so you can keep the problem manageable and in proportion. If you find it difficult to contain the effect of a conflict in the rest of your life, you might deal with this in several ways:

- Try to bring the roots of the conflict out into the open, if you feel a discussion about what's wrong might help to resolve the problem.

- Do visualizations to help yourself detach from the conflict and use them to remind yourself that this conflict is confined to only one part of your life; it shouldn't slide over into other areas.

- Remove yourself from the conflict situation if other alternatives don't work.

- Cut the conflict down to size by getting rid of the day-to-day input that feeds the bad feelings and thoughts about the conflict in your mind. For example, do not record information about the conflict in a journal; turn your thoughts to something else if the history of the conflict comes to mind; do not rehearse what you plan to say to the person with whom you are in conflict in future conversations.

One typical situation where some or all of these strategies might be appropriate is when there is a personality clash between people in an office. Imagine that a few people don't like each other; the atmosphere feels tense as they work together. Overt expressions of conflict are infrequent and only last for a few minutes. But the feelings triggered by these encounters can grow and grow. They not only poison the working environment, but employees often take those feelings home with them. Then those feelings at home can trigger all sorts of petty irritations that can erupt into further conflicts, such as with spouses and children. Then *they* become upset and hostile. So the bad feelings and conflicts spread even more. It's like an infection that spreads and spreads from one person to another. Hence, a single conflict is sometimes like a seed that germinates or disease germ that spreads, growing and passing on more and more bad feelings and thoughts.

Thus, as soon as you see the effects of a conflict spreading, implement a strategy of containment. Keep the conflict to one area and one issue; do what you can to resolve it. Learn from it if you can, then put it away and move on.

As you work to bring a conflict down to size, a visualization might help. For instance, see the tentacles of the conflict reaching out from the center of the original conflict; see the new shoots of growth, or the new invasions of disease being chopped off. As you imagine this cutting off or containment, think about some of the key principles for keeping a conflict in proportion. Repeat them mentally again and again, as an affirmation, keeping the conflict down to size.

Some key principles to keep a conflict in proportion include these:

- *Don't let a bad experience deflect you from your overall purpose or direction.* The conflict may suggest you need to make a slight correction or improve what you are doing in some way. But you can, and should, keep on going. See the experience as a challenge or stepping stone to guide you in a new direction.

- *Find your center or purpose and remain firmly committed to that; don't let other people's attitudes and expectations throw you off.* This reminder is especially relevant to conflicts that arise out of differences in values and goals. At times, you might find yourself thrown off-kilter by confronting someone's views about what you should or shouldn't do. While it helps to recognize and respect different perspectives, keep your own focus in mind, too; don't let someone else's ideas displace your own.

- *Don't let a conflict or bad experience undermine your self-confidence and self-esteem.* It can sometimes be easy to feel unnerved after a conflict, especially if you feel you have lost something or have given in to settle the conflict. But try to disconnect yourself from the conflict, and don't invest your self-worth in winning the conflict. The outcome of a conflict doesn't change who you are. It's something that happened, and when it's over and resolved, it's time to move on. Remember that the deflation of self-confidence which sometimes occurs in a conflict is just a passing feeling triggered by the event. This will help you put the experience back in perspective. It's like the old gospel favorite sung by the late Johnny Cash, "These Things Shall Pass." If you remind yourself of that when you're starting to let a conflict get to you, you'll feel better about yourself right away.

- *Remind yourself that a conflict is just a small percentage of your many experiences.* It's just a small part of the sum total of the many things you are doing. Right after a conflict, you may tend to magnify its importance and focus on the bad feelings that linger. You lose sight of the positives or lessons that might come out of it if you think about the conflict creatively. Accordingly, remind yourself that in time the conflict will sink back into its proper perspective among the many other things happening in your life. You just have to be willing to process it, learn what you can from it, and let it go.

Overcoming Negative Feelings

Sometimes it can be hard to find ways to learn from a conflict or put the conflict experience in perspective because of the bad feelings due to the conflict. Thinking about how you can gain from a conflict or shrink it down in size often will get rid of those bad feelings. But if that doesn't happen, you may need to take some steps to let go of your feelings before you can put the conflict in perspective or learn from it.

While time will diffuse many or all of these feelings, the following suggestions are designed to speed up this process of letting go.

• *Forgive yourself.* One common reason for feeling bad after a conflict is having feelings of self-blame. You feel what happened was your own fault, or you feel you might have acted differently to produce a more positive outcome. But the problem with these recriminations and regrets is the event is over and you can't change it now. All you are doing is making yourself feel bad. Thus, if you catch yourself blaming yourself or thinking, "I wish I had done that differently; I know I could have; why didn't I?"—short-circuit the process and stop the blaming. Instead of blaming, learn to forgive yourself. For instance, tell yourself what you feel you did wrong in initiating, participating in, or resolving the conflict. Then for each wrong, tell yourself: "I forgive."

• *Vent your feelings.* Besides feelings of blame which require forgiving, you may have other feelings left over from a conflict that are difficult to get rid of. And you may find that thinking rationally about the conflict being over and done just isn't enough; the feelings remain. For example, though you have reached an agreement or compromise, you feel so hostile that the conflict might erupt again. Or you may feel discouraged and drained or generally upset because of the battle. Whatever your negative feelings, it helps to express and vent those feelings, so you can let them go. One way to do this might be to write about what happened in a journal or talk about your experience into a cassette recorder. Another possibility is to find a quiet time to meditate, reflect on what happened, and notice the bad feelings that arise. Then, using your powers to visualize, see yourself putting those feelings into a sack. See yourself take that sack outside somewhere. Bury that sack in the ground or burn it up, so those feelings will never again bother you. Through venting, you express and use up those feelings. Once free of them, you can go back and look at ways to work with or learn from the conflict in a more productive way.

• *Recognize that others may be less critical than you think.* Sometimes you may think that people are blaming you for what happened or that you showed a not-so-attractive side of yourself, and you suffer a drop in self-esteem. One way to deal with this concern with others' judgment is to recognize that other people may be less critical of what you did than you are. That's because you may have much higher standards than others, since you are judging yourself and your own ego is on the line. Then, too, it can sometimes help to talk to the people you feel have bad feelings about you or the situation. You may find they don't have the negative feelings you feared after all. Even if they do, you can make any necessary apologies or explanations, and thereby smooth away those negative feelings. Other people can be critical, but they should recognize and accept your humanness, which includes sometimes making mistakes.

- *Do something to take your mind off your feelings.* Finally, a good way to break out of the cycle of negative feelings is to do something active or physical. This will focus your mind on something else, and the shift in attention will help to dispel your negative feelings. Spend a few hours on an involving work project; go to a movie; make or eat a food dish you enjoy; talk to a friend; plan a trip you might take. Whatever you do, the action should take all your attention. This will help stop your obsessing about the conflict and make your negative feelings fade away. And if you can't sleep because you keep reviewing a conflict that just happened, don't lie there and try to force sleep to come to you. Get up and tackle something you've been avoiding; you might clean up the papers on your desk. Look at a late night movie on TV, or try reading a book or magazine in your pile of things to read.

Don't Let Others Hold You Back

One trap that can keep you from dealing with a conflict situation creatively is the attitude of other people. Sometimes they have a preconceived view of what you are or what you have done, which differs from your view. This fact may have contributed to the conflict, and even after the conflict is over, that limiting view may continue to influence you. If so, you need to shake off that view. The first step is becoming aware that this viewpoint it is having a negative influence on you. Then you must work on freeing yourself from the tyranny of other people's opinions, especially the negative, self-defeating ones. The following ways of dealing with others can help you shake off other people's negativity.

Avoid negative people who won't change. When a speaker gives a speech, he or she can easily be thrown off track by a negative, disapproving person. Some speakers get so concerned about proving themselves to this person that they drain themselves of energy, losing the people who were positive and accepting.

It is the same in a conflict situation. You may find yourself battling with someone with a different point of view. Sometimes it helps to look at how this person sees things; by feeling and expressing empathy for the other's point of view, you may find a win-win resolution the other person can accept. But there is a danger in doing this: You don't want to go so far in looking at things from the other side that you forget your own perspective. If so, you may find yourself accommodating the other person by giving up what you really value, because you have let the other person's view of yourself and your opinions put you down.

If you see this happening, it may be better to pull away from the situation. Ask yourself if there is any point in struggling to change the opinions of negative people. Their mind may already be made up and they may be set in their disapproval. If so, why struggle against it? If you can shift them around by a clear presentation of objective facts, fine. If not, let the conflict go and move on. Just as a speaker is wise to let a few hecklers go to please the rest of the audience, you will get further if you focus on the people who are supportive and accepting of your viewpoint. So where possible, concentrate on relating to them.

Don't waste energy on skeptics who won't listen. Just as you can deflate yourself by trying to get the approval of someone who is determined to be negative and disapproving towards you, you can spin your wheels trying to convince someone who is skeptical and antagonistic to your viewpoint. Of course, it can be valuable to have an honest and open discussion with such a person, because by sharing views you can both get ideas. But if after awhile you see that someone still holds rigidly to skeptical or critical views and you just as strongly believe in what you are thinking or doing, it's probably best to stop trying to convince the person. If you keep trying, your efforts are likely to lead to an open conflict; the person won't be convinced, and you are apt to end up feeling drained of your energy, angry, hostile, or worse.

Such a conflict may only prove to be a quagmire that sucks you in deeper, undermining your sense of confidence and faith. That's not the kind of conflict from which you can learn and grow. The moral: Be on your guard against die-hard skeptics and critics who don't seek to learn anything from sharing of ideas with you and only want to prove they are right.

Don't let others guilt-trip you. Another way that others can block you from dealing constructively with a conflict is by making you feel guilty when you are aware of their condemnation or disapproval for something you did or something they believe you did. This block is much like the self-blame hurdle described earlier, which requires self-forgiveness to overcome. The main difference here is that you are not blaming yourself; you're taking on the perspective of others who you think are blaming you.

Freeing yourself of this perceived blame and your resulting guilty feelings requires two steps. First, get rid of this other perspective and stop trying to see yourself through others' eyes. Second, let go of the blame and the guilt. You might accomplish both by questioning what right others have to judge you or evaluate your worth. They don't see the whole you, made up of many motivations, interests, and needs, so they can't fully understand you. There's even less reason for you to judge yourself by what you think others think, since not only may they be wrong in judging you, but you may be wrong in judging their judgments of you. You can see how confounded all this can get, so distance yourself from any judgments by others, which are often as unknowable as they are unfounded.

If feelings of fault and guilt remain, even after you have released yourself from the view of others, free yourself through forgiveness. A gesture, expression, or ritual of forgiveness may help you do this. Or use a visual image, such as cleansing yourself of guilt in a purifying lake, seeing an object representing your guilt shattering or burning up, or imagining yourself being forgiven by an authority figure, teacher, or spiritual guide.

Releasing Negative Feelings and Moving On

Still another potential block to moving on creatively and productively after a conflict is having bad feelings over the disruptions in personal relationships caused by the conflict. It can be necessary to release these feelings before you can move on to look at the conflict constructively with an eye towards the future.

One key to this release is being ready to talk to others who you feel have leftover bad feelings about something that occurred, (e.g., if you feel they are still angry, have lost respect for you, or think you took advantage of them). If you follow up and talk to these people a few days after the conflict occurred (giving things a little time to settle), you may find they don't have these lingering bad feelings towards you after all. Maybe you just imagined that they did because you were feeling that about yourself. Or if they do still have lingering feelings, you may be able to smooth the relationship over by showing your concern. This smoothing over can contribute to feeling finished about the conflict and looking at it more objectively, so you can learn from it and move on.

At the same time, if you have bad feelings about what happened, and are still angry, feel someone took advantage of you, or have lost respect for another person, you also need to release those feelings to move on. Sometimes it can be helpful to talk over your reactions with the other person to clear the air, if the other person is receptive to discussing the issue. At other times, it can be better to just work on letting go of your own negative feelings, so you don't escalate the conflict by trying to talk about it while feelings on both sides are raw, or if the other person doesn't like to talk about problems. If you do need to simply let go and release, you might use some of the visualization techniques discussed in Chapters 2 and 6 to help you get rid of any post-conflict negative feelings so that you can move on.

Summing Up

You can help turn your conflicts into creative opportunities by remembering the following:

1. Look at the conflict to see what you can learn.

2. Go within yourself to get ideas on how to benefit and learn from your bad experience.

3. Keep your conflicts in proportion by doing the following:

   a. Don't let a bad experience deflect you from your overall purpose or direction.

   b. Find your own center or purpose and come from that; don't let other people's attitudes and expectations throw you off.

   c. Don't let a conflict or bad experience undermine your feelings of self-confidence and self-esteem.

   d. Remind yourself that a conflict is just a small percentage of your many experiences.

4. Overcome your negative feelings after a conflict through the following methods:

   a. Learn to forgive yourself.

   b. Take some time to vent your feelings.

    c. Recognize that other people may be less critical of you or of what happened than you are.

    d. Talk to the other party, if the other party is receptive and you can do so calmly and comfortably, so you each get your feelings and concerns out in the open. Then you may be able to forgive or reconcile, so you can both move on.

5. Avoid the block of letting others hold you back.

    a. Be careful to avoid being sucked in by people who are negative or disapproving of what you are doing; focus on people who are positive and accepting.

    b. Don't put too much energy into trying to convince the skeptics if they don't want to listen.

    c. Don't let others make you feel guilty for something you haven't done—or even for something you have.

    d. Be ready to talk to others whom you feel may have bad feelings lingering on after a conflict, so you can get rid of any misconceptions or smooth over any bad feelings.

Index

About the Author

Gini Graham Scott, Ph.D., JD, is a nationally known writer, consultant, speaker, and seminar/workshop leader, specializing in business and work relationships, and professional and personal development. She is founder and director of Changemakers, and has published more than forty books on diverse subjects. Her previous books on business relationships and professional development include: *A Survival Guide to Managing Employees from Hell, A Survival Guide for Working with Bad Bosses, A Survival Guide for Working with Humans, Resolving Conflict,* and *Work with Me! Resolving Everyday Conflict in Your Organization.* Her books on professional and personal development include *30 Days to a More Powerful Memory, The Empowered Mind: How to Harness the Creative Force Within You* and *Mind Power: Picture Your Way to Success.*

Scott has received national media exposure for her books, including appearances on *Good Morning America!, Oprah, Geraldo at Large, Montel Williams,* CNN, and *The O'Reilly Factor.* She has written a dozen screenplays, several signed to agents or optioned by producers, and is the executive producer of a small film production company, Changemakers Productions. She is also a game designer, with more than two dozen games on the market with major game companies, including Hasbro, Pressman, and Mag-Nif. Two new games were introduced by Briarpatch in 2007: *Jackpot* and *Do You Look Like Your Dog?,* based on the book and Web site of the same name.

She has taught classes at several colleges, including California State University East Bay, Notre Dame de Namur University, and the Investigative Career Program in San Francisco. She received a Ph.D. in Sociology from the University of California in Berkeley, a JD from the University of San Francisco Law School, and MAs in Anthropology, Mass Communications, and Organizational, Consumer, and Audience Behavior from Cal State University, East Bay. She will be receiving an additional MA in Popular Culture and Lifestyles in 2007.

She is also the founder and director of MakingConnections.biz, which has a network of services connecting clients with the publishing, film, music, game and toy, speaking, and venture capital industries and the media. The five-year old service has served almost 1,000 clients, and has been written up in the *Wall Street Journal* and other publications.

For more information, you can visit her websites at www.gini grahamscott.com, which includes a video of media clips and speaking engagements, and www.giniscott.com, which features her books. Or contact her company at:

Changemakers
6114 La Salle, #358
Oakland, CA 94611
(510) 339–1625
changemakers@pacbell.net